*Christ Revealed*

# Christ Revealed

Tony Medley

Title: *Christ Fully Revealed*
Author: Dr. Tony E. Medley Sr.

Published by Medley Publishing Group
Printed in the United States of America

ISBN (Paperback): 979-8-9940033-5-0
ISBN (eBook): 979-8-9940033-6-7

Unless otherwise indicated, Scripture quotations are taken from the Holy Bible. Emphasis within Scripture quotations (italics, bold, capitalization) has been added by the author.

This work is intended for educational and instructional purposes in biblical studies and Christian education. It is not intended to replace personal study of Scripture, pastoral guidance, or academic advisement.

Cover design and interior layout by Dr. Tony E. Medley Sr.

# Dedication

To students, who have accepted the call to study God's Word deeply, that you may be equipped for ministry and faithful service in the Kingdom of God.

And to my family, whose love and support strengthen me daily.

This work is also dedicated to all who hunger and thirst after righteousness—

may the Word of God be your bread and your life.

# *Preface*

The Old Testament Survey Study Guide was written to provide students with a clear, accessible, and spiritually nourishing introduction to the 39 books of the Old Testament.

As believers, we often focus heavily on the New Testament, yet the Old Testament forms the foundation of our faith. It introduces us to God as Creator, Covenant-Keeper, Judge, Redeemer, and King. It tells the story of Israel—chosen, redeemed, disciplined, and restored—and through its pages, it points us forward to Christ, the promised Messiah.

This study guide is designed not only to provide historical and literary background, but also to serve as a devotional companion. Each chapter includes:

- A background summary,
- Expository lessons,
- Themes and theological insights,
- A Christ-centered connection,
- Memory verses, and
- Reflection questions.

My prayer is that this book will strengthen your faith, sharpen your understanding, and equip you to teach others also. May it inspire you to love God's Word more deeply and live it more faithfully.

DR. TONY E. MEDLEY SR.

# *Acknowledgments*

I want to acknowledge and thank:

- The Lord Jesus Christ, the Living Word, whose Spirit has guided every page.
- My family, who have encouraged and supported me through countless hours of study and writing.
- The students, whose hunger for truth and commitment to ministry inspired this work.

Finally, I am indebted to the generations of faithful teachers, pastors, and scholars who have taught me the Scriptures and shown me that every word of God is trustworthy.

# Genesis

As we begin our journey through the Old Testament, I want you to pause and think about this: every great story has a beginning. The book of Genesis is not just the beginning of the Bible—it is the beginning of everything: the world, humanity, family, nations, sin, and God's plan of redemption. When you open Genesis, you are standing at the doorway of God's grand design, looking into His heart, His creativity, and His covenant love.

Too often, people read Genesis as though it is only an ancient history book, but I want you to see it as our family history, the roots of our faith, the place where God first reveals who He is and how He relates to His people. Genesis lays the foundation for every other book in the Bible. Without it, we would not understand God's covenant with Abraham, the importance of Israel, or even why we need Jesus Christ as our Savior.

Let us take this chapter slowly, as if we are walking step by step with Adam, Noah, Abraham, Isaac, Jacob, and Joseph. Let their stories come alive, not as distant characters, but as our spiritual ancestors whose lives reveal God's faithfulness and humanity's constant need for grace.

## Background of Genesis

Genesis was traditionally written by Moses, likely during Israel's wilderness years. Its name means "beginnings" or "origins." It records the span of time from creation itself through the death of Joseph in Egypt.

But Genesis is more than a collection of stories. It is God's revelation. It explains the origin of sin, the brokenness of the world, and God's plan to bless all nations through Abraham's descendants.

## Outline of Genesis

1. Creation and Early Humanity (Chapters 1–11)
   ◦ God creates the world and everything in it.
   ◦ Humanity falls into sin and experiences judgment (the Fall, the Flood, Babel).
   ◦ Yet, God continues to show mercy and keeps the promise of redemption alive.
2. The Patriarchs (Chapters 12–50)
   ◦ Abraham is called to walk by faith and receives the covenant promises.
   ◦ Isaac carries forward God's promises despite being a quiet figure.
   ◦ Jacob wrestles with God and is transformed into Israel, father of the twelve tribes.
   ◦ Joseph is betrayed, enslaved, and exalted, showing God's providence.

This structure helps us see that Genesis moves from a universal scope (all of humanity) to a narrow focus (God's chosen family). God begins with the world and narrows His plan through Abraham's line, setting the stage for the coming Messiah.

## Themes of Genesis

1. Creation: God is sovereign Creator, and all He makes is good.
2. Sin: Humanity rebels, bringing judgment and separation.

3. Covenant: God promises blessing and redemption through Abraham's family.
4. Providence: God works behind the scenes to accomplish His plan.

Each of these themes will appear again throughout the Bible, but Genesis introduces them with clarity.

### Key Figures and Lessons

- Adam and Eve: Their disobedience shows us the seriousness of sin and our desperate need for redemption. Yet, God clothed them, pointing to His mercy.
- Noah: Faithful obedience in a corrupt world; his story reminds us that one person's faithfulness matters.
- Abraham: Called to leave everything behind, he becomes the father of faith. His journey shows that righteousness comes through faith, not works.
- Jacob: A deceiver transformed by God's grace into Israel. His story reminds us that God uses flawed people.
- Joseph: Betrayed by his brothers, yet elevated to save many lives. His story reveals God's providence and points us to Jesus, who also suffered but was exalted to save us.

### Christ in Genesis

Genesis whispers Christ's name again and again:

- The Seed of the Woman (Genesis 3:15) – the first prophecy of Jesus' victory over Satan.
- Melchizedek – a king-priest figure, foreshadowing Jesus as our eternal High Priest.

- The near-sacrifice of Isaac – foreshadows God giving His only Son.
- Joseph's story – betrayal, suffering, and exaltation mirror Jesus' path.

Genesis is not just history—it is a prophetic book pointing straight to the cross.

## Memory Verse

Genesis 12:2–3 – "I will make you into a great nation, and I will bless you; I will make your name great, and you will be a blessing... and all peoples on earth will be blessed through you."

This verse captures God's mission: Abraham's family was chosen not just for themselves, but to bless the whole world—a promise fulfilled in Christ.

## Reflection Questions

1. How does Genesis 1–2 shape our understanding of God as Creator?
2. What hope does Genesis 3:15 give us after the Fall?
3. Why do you think God chose Abraham, and what does his faith teach us?
4. How does Joseph's story encourage you to trust God in difficult circumstances?

## Final Thoughts from the Author

Genesis is not just about "where we came from." It is about who God is and how He acts in history. It shows us that even when humanity sins, God's plan of redemption cannot be stopped. When you study Genesis, don't just memorize dates and names—listen for the heartbeat of God. Hear Him calling humanity back to Himself.

My prayer is that as you read Genesis, you will see your own life reflected in its pages: your struggles in Adam and Eve, your doubts in Abraham, your transformation in Jacob, and your hope in Joseph. And above all, may you see Jesus Christ, the promised Seed, shining through every chapter.

# { 2 }

# Exodus

When we turn the pages from Genesis to Exodus, we are not stepping into a new story but into the continuation of God's great redemptive plan. Genesis closed with Jacob's family settled in Egypt under Joseph's favor. Exodus begins four centuries later, with that same family grown into a nation but shackled in chains of slavery. What happened? The new Pharaoh "did not know Joseph" (Exodus 1:8), and what began as blessing became bondage.

Exodus is the book of redemption, the story of God's mighty hand reaching down to free His people. But it is more than history—it is theology in action. Exodus shows us what salvation looks like: God hears, God delivers, God covenants, and God dwells with His people. Let us walk through this sacred book step by step, as though sitting under Moses' teaching.

## God's People in Bondage (Exodus 1–2)

Exodus opens with Israel enslaved in Egypt. Their cries ascend to heaven, and God hears them. Notice Exodus 2:24–25: "God heard their groaning, and God remembered his covenant with Abraham, with Isaac, and with Jacob. God saw the people of Israel—and God knew."

This is no distant deity. He is the covenant-keeping God. Four verbs stand out: He heard, He remembered, He saw, He knew. This is the God we serve—intimately aware of our suffering.

Into this setting God raises up Moses, preserved as an infant, trained in Pharaoh's courts, humbled in the wilderness, and called from the burning bush (Exodus 3). God reveals His name: "I AM WHO I AM" (Yahweh), the eternal, self-existent One. This name anchors Israel's faith and assures us that God's promises never expire.

## God's Mighty Deliverance (Exodus 3–15)

Pharaoh's heart was hard, but God's hand was strong. Through ten plagues, Yahweh demonstrates His supremacy over Egypt's so-called gods. Every plague is not random—it is targeted. The Nile turned to blood mocked the river god; darkness defied the sun god; the death of the firstborn struck at Pharaoh himself, who claimed divine sonship.

At the heart of this section lies the Passover (Exodus 12). God instructs Israel to sacrifice a spotless lamb and apply its blood to the doorposts. The destroyer would "pass over" every house marked by the blood. This is salvation by substitution: one dies so another may live. Does that sound familiar? Yes, here in Exodus we see the shadow of Calvary, where Christ our Passover was sacrificed for us (1 Cor. 5:7).

The climax of deliverance comes at the Red Sea (Exodus 14). Israel trapped between Pharaoh's army and the waters learns the eternal truth: "The LORD will fight for you; you need only to be still" (Exodus 14:14). God parts the sea, Israel walks on dry land, and Pharaoh's army is drowned. This crossing becomes the defining act of salvation for Israel, referenced throughout the Old Testament as proof of God's redeeming power.

## God's Covenant at Sinai (Exodus 19-24)

Redemption leads to relationship. God did not just bring Israel out of Egypt—He brought them to Himself at Mount Sinai. Exodus 19:4 declares: "I bore you on eagles' wings and brought you to myself."

Here God enters into covenant with His people. He gives the Ten Commandments (Exodus 20), not as burdens but as boundaries of love. Notice the order: before God gives law, He reminds them of grace—"I am the LORD your God, who brought you out of Egypt." Law comes after redemption, not before. Obedience is the response to salvation, never the cause.

The Ten Commandments cover two great relationships: love for God (commands 1–4) and love for neighbor (commands 5–10). Jesus later summarized them in Matthew 22:37–40: love God with all your heart, and love your neighbor as yourself.

## God's Presence in the Tabernacle (Exodus 25-40)

The second half of Exodus may seem tedious with its detailed instructions for building the Tabernacle, but do not overlook its significance. The Tabernacle is God's dwelling place among His people. This is revolutionary! The holy God of heaven comes down to live in the midst of His redeemed people.

Every detail of the Tabernacle points to Christ:

- The Ark of the Covenant reminds us of God's throne of grace.
- The altar of sacrifice foreshadows the cross.
- The lampstand points to Christ as the Light of the World.
- The bread of the presence speaks of Christ as the Bread of Life.

When the Tabernacle was completed, "the glory of the LORD filled the tabernacle" (Exodus 40:34). God's presence was no longer distant; He was with them. This anticipates John 1:14: "The Word became flesh and dwelt among us." The Hebrew idea of "dwelt" literally means "tabernacled." Christ is the fulfillment of God's presence with His people.

## Christ in Exodus

Exodus is one of the clearest foreshadowings of Christ in all of Scripture:

- Moses as the mediator prefigures Christ, our greater Mediator.
- The Passover Lamb points to Christ's atoning death.
- The Red Sea crossing symbolizes our baptism into new life.
- The Law at Sinai shows us our need for grace fulfilled in Christ.
- The Tabernacle is fulfilled in Christ's incarnation and presence with His church.

## Memory Verse

Exodus 14:13–14 – "Fear not, stand firm, and see the salvation of the LORD, which He will work for you today... The LORD will fight for you, and you have only to be silent."

## Reflection Questions

1. What do the plagues reveal about God's power and Egypt's false gods?
2. How does the Passover foreshadow the work of Christ on the cross?
3. Why is it important that the Ten Commandments come after God's act of redemption?
4. How do the details of the Tabernacle point us to Jesus?
5. In what ways do you experience God's presence as your "dwelling place" today?

## Final Exhortation

Exodus teaches us that salvation is not only deliverance from sin but also deliverance to worship, obedience, and God's presence. If God has redeemed you, He has also called you into covenant and communion with Himself.

Remember, dear students, the God of Exodus is your God today. He still hears, still delivers, still covenants, and still dwells with His people. As you study Exodus, let your heart echo Israel's song at the sea: "The LORD is my strength and my song; He has become my salvation" (Exodus 15:2).

# { 3 }

# Leviticus

Many readers skip over the book of Leviticus because they find its laws strange, its sacrifices repetitive, and its details overwhelming. But I urge you—do not overlook this sacred text. Leviticus is the heartbeat of holiness. It answers the question: How can a sinful people dwell in the presence of a holy God?

Exodus ended with God's glory filling the Tabernacle (Exodus 40:34). Leviticus opens by showing us how Israel can approach that glory without being consumed. If Genesis is about beginnings, and Exodus about redemption, then Leviticus is about sanctification—living as God's holy people.

Let us walk together, verse by verse and theme by theme, to see how Leviticus is not an ancient manual of rituals, but a prophetic picture of Christ and a call to holiness that still speaks to us today.

## The Structure of Leviticus

Leviticus can be divided into three major sections:

1. Sacrificial Laws (Chapters 1–7)
    ◦ The burnt offering, grain offering, peace offering, sin offering, and guilt offering.
    ◦ Each teaches that sin must be atoned for and fellowship with God restored.
2. Priestly Laws (Chapters 8–10)

- ∘ The consecration of Aaron and his sons as priests.
- ∘ The sobering story of Nadab and Abihu, struck down for offering "strange fire."
3. Laws of Holiness (Chapters 11–27)
   - ∘ Clean and unclean foods, purity laws, the Day of Atonement.
   - ∘ Holiness code for Israel's moral, social, and spiritual life.
   - ∘ Festivals that mark Israel's calendar of worship.

## Key Themes of Leviticus

1. Holiness: God declares, "Be holy, for I am holy" (Lev. 19:2). Holiness is not optional—it is God's calling for His people.
2. Sacrifice: Sin separates, but blood atones. Every offering pointed forward to Christ's perfect sacrifice.
3. Priesthood: Israel needed mediators to stand between them and God. Christ is now our Great High Priest.
4. Presence: God desires to dwell among His people in purity, not compromise.
5. Worship: Worship is not casual—it is regulated by God, not invented by man.

## The Sacrificial System (Leviticus 1–7)

Each sacrifice teaches us something about sin and salvation:

- Burnt Offering (Ch. 1): Total devotion—Christ offered Himself fully to God.
- Grain Offering (Ch. 2): Thanksgiving—points to Christ as the Bread of Life.
- Peace Offering (Ch. 3): Fellowship—points to reconciliation in Christ.
- Sin Offering (Ch. 4): Atonement for unintentional sin.

- Guilt Offering (Ch. 5–7): Restitution for sin against God or others.

Every drop of blood cried out that sin is deadly serious. Hebrews 9:22 echoes: "Without the shedding of blood there is no forgiveness." Yet these sacrifices were shadows; Christ is the substance.

## The Priesthood (Leviticus 8–10)

God sets apart Aaron and his sons as priests. They were clothed in holy garments, anointed with oil, and consecrated to serve. But priesthood came with danger. Nadab and Abihu offered unauthorized fire, and fire from the Lord consumed them (Lev. 10:1–2).

This is a sobering reminder: God is not to be approached on our own terms. Worship must be according to His Word, not human invention. Today, Christ is our High Priest (Hebrews 4:14–16), and we too are called "a royal priesthood" (1 Peter 2:9), offering spiritual sacrifices acceptable to God.

## Purity and the Day of Atonement (Leviticus 11–16)

Chapters 11–15 lay out laws of purity—foods, diseases, bodily discharges. These may feel foreign, but they remind us that sin corrupts and holiness separates. Israel's daily life was meant to reflect their distinct identity as God's people.

At the heart of Leviticus is the Day of Atonement (Yom Kippur, Ch. 16). Once a year, the high priest entered the Holy of Holies, sprinkling blood on the mercy seat for the sins of the people. Two goats were chosen: one sacrificed, the other (the scapegoat) sent into the wilderness, symbolically carrying away Israel's sins.

This points directly to Christ: He is both the sacrifice that atones and the scapegoat who removes our sins "as far as the east is from the west" (Psalm 103:12). Hebrews 10:14 declares: "By one sacrifice He has perfected forever those who are being sanctified."

## The Holiness Code and Festivals (Leviticus 17–27)

Here God teaches His people how to live as a holy nation:

- Moral laws: Sexual purity, honesty, care for the poor, justice in society.
- Worship laws: No idolatry, proper sacrifices, reverence for God's name.
- Festivals: Passover, Unleavened Bread, Firstfruits, Pentecost, Trumpets, Day of Atonement, and Tabernacles. Each festival pointed to Christ's saving work and God's plan of redemption.

Leviticus closes with blessings for obedience and curses for disobedience, reminding Israel that holiness brings life, while rebellion brings ruin.

## Christ in Leviticus

- Christ is the spotless sacrifice, fulfilling every offering.
- Christ is the High Priest, entering once for all into the heavenly sanctuary.
- Christ is our Scapegoat, carrying away our sins.
- Christ is the Holy One, making His people holy.
- Christ is the rest of the Sabbath and the fulfillment of every feast.

Leviticus teaches us that holiness is not about rituals but about Christ Himself, who sanctifies us completely.

## Memory Verse

Leviticus 19:2 – "You shall be holy, for I the LORD your God am holy."

## Reflection Questions

1. Why did God require blood sacrifices in Israel's worship?
2. How does the Day of Atonement point directly to Jesus Christ?
3. What lessons can we learn from the story of Nadab and Abihu?
4. How does Leviticus teach us that holiness touches every area of life—family, work, society, and worship?
5. How can we live as a "holy priesthood" today in light of 1 Peter 2:9?

## Final Exhortation

Students, Leviticus may seem hard at first, but it is a book we desperately need. In a world that trivializes sin and mocks holiness, Leviticus reminds us that God is holy and His people must be holy.

Yet holiness is not about rules—it is about relationship. God calls us to Himself, not just to follow commands but to walk in covenant love. The sacrifices and rituals were temporary pictures of the ultimate sacrifice—Jesus Christ, who makes us holy.

As you study Leviticus, do not just see restrictions. See the love of a holy God who longs to dwell with His people. Hear His voice calling you: "Be holy, for I am holy." And remember, the same God who commands holiness also provides it through the blood of His Son.

# { 4 }

# Numbers

As we move into the book of Numbers, we encounter a sobering reality: God had redeemed His people from Egypt, given them His covenant at Sinai, and promised them the land of Canaan—but they failed to believe. Numbers is a book about testing, rebellion, and the consequences of unbelief. Yet, it also reveals God's patience and faithfulness.

The Hebrew title of Numbers is Bemidbar, meaning "In the Wilderness." This is fitting, for the wilderness is the setting where Israel's faith was tried and often failed. The English title "Numbers" comes from the censuses recorded in chapters 1 and 26, bookends of a generation lost and another prepared.

If Exodus shows us redemption, and Leviticus holiness, then Numbers teaches us about the journey of faith—with its trials, dangers, and God's sustaining presence.

## The Structure of Numbers

1. Preparation at Sinai (Ch. 1–10)
     ◦ Census of tribes and arrangement of the camp
     ◦ Laws for purity and worship
     ◦ Dedication of Levites
     ◦ Cloud of God's presence leads them
2. Failure in the Wilderness (Ch. 11–25)
     ◦ Complaints about food and leadership

- Rebellion of Miriam and Aaron
- The spies and unbelief at Kadesh-Barnea
- Forty years of wandering pronounced
- Korah's rebellion and further complaints
- Balaam's prophecies

3. Preparation for the Promised Land (Ch. 26–36)
    - Second census of a new generation
    - Laws for inheritance and offerings
    - Victory over Midian
    - Boundaries of the land
    - Cities of refuge established

### Key Themes of Numbers

1. Faith vs. Unbelief: God's promises are sure, but unbelief leads to wandering.
2. Leadership and Rebellion: God raises leaders, but His people often resist them.
3. God's Holiness: Disobedience brings judgment, but God remains faithful.
4. God's Presence: Even in rebellion, God never abandons His people.
5. Hope for a New Generation: Though one generation falls, God prepares another to receive His promises.

### Key Events and Lessons

- The Census (Ch. 1–2): Israel is numbered and arranged, showing God's order. Every tribe has a place; God is at the center. What a picture of the church—many members, one body, Christ at the center.
- The Complaints Begin (Ch. 11): Israel longs for Egypt's food. How quickly we forget God's deliverance when our appetites

rule us! God provides manna, but their craving leads to judgment.

- The Spies and Unbelief (Ch. 13–14): Twelve spies are sent; ten bring fear, two bring faith (Joshua and Caleb). Israel believes the fearful report and refuses to enter the land. God sentences them to wander forty years, until the unbelieving generation dies. The lesson? Faith looks at God's promises, not the size of the giants.
- Korah's Rebellion (Ch. 16): Leaders rise up against Moses and Aaron, claiming all are equal. God affirms His chosen servants by opening the earth to swallow the rebels. Leadership is God's calling, not man's ambition.
- Moses' Disobedience (Ch. 20): In anger, Moses strikes the rock instead of speaking to it. Though water flows, Moses dishonors God's holiness and is barred from entering the land. Even great leaders are accountable to God.
- The Bronze Serpent (Ch. 21): When the people complain, God sends fiery serpents. Yet He also provides healing—those who look at the bronze serpent live. Jesus applies this in John 3:14–15: just as the serpent was lifted up, so must the Son of Man be lifted up, that whoever believes may have eternal life.
- Balaam's Prophecy (Ch. 22–24): Though hired to curse Israel, Balaam can only bless them, even foretelling a future star and scepter (a prophecy of Christ, Num. 24:17).

## Key Lessons from Numbers

1. Unbelief has consequences. A whole generation perished because they doubted God's promise.
2. Leadership is tested. Moses, Aaron, and Joshua faced constant opposition, but God vindicated His servants.
3. Sin spreads. Complaining, rebellion, and idolatry affect the whole community.

4. God is faithful. Though Israel was unfaithful, God preserved a new generation and prepared them to inherit the land.
5. Christ is the remedy. The bronze serpent points us to the cross, where faith in Christ brings healing from sin's curse.

## Christ in Numbers

- The Rock that gave water (20:8–11) points to Christ, the living water (1 Cor. 10:4).
- The Bronze Serpent (21:8–9) foreshadows Christ on the cross (John 3:14–15).
- The Star and Scepter prophecy (24:17) predicts Christ as King.
- Moses as mediator points to Christ, our greater Mediator.

Numbers reminds us that Christ is our provision in the wilderness and our hope for the Promised Land.

## Memory Verse

Numbers 23:19 – "God is not man, that He should lie, or a son of man, that He should change His mind. Has He said, and will He not do it? Or has He spoken, and will He not fulfill it?"

This verse anchors our faith: God's promises are unshakable.

## Reflection Questions

1. What does Israel's unbelief at Kadesh-Barnea teach us about trusting God's promises?
2. Why do you think complaining is such a serious sin in God's eyes?
3. What lessons do we learn from Moses' disobedience at Meribah?
4. How does the bronze serpent point to the cross of Christ?

5. In what ways can we live as people who trust God's promises today?

## Final Exhortation

Students, Numbers is a warning and an encouragement. It warns us not to harden our hearts in unbelief (Hebrews 3:7–19). But it also encourages us that even in our failures, God remains faithful.

You may feel like you are wandering in your own wilderness—discouraged, doubting, or weary. Remember this: God does not abandon His people. His presence was with Israel in the cloud and fire; His presence is with us in Christ through the Holy Spirit.

Let us be like Joshua and Caleb, men of a different spirit, who believed God when others doubted. For faith sees the giants, but also sees the God who is greater. Faith says, "We are well able to overcome" (Num. 13:30).

Walk in faith, dear students. Do not die in the wilderness of unbelief when God has promised you the inheritance of His kingdom.

# { 5 }

# Deuteronomy

We have walked through Genesis (beginnings), Exodus (redemption), Leviticus (holiness), and Numbers (testing). Now we come to Deuteronomy, the great book of renewal and remembrance.

The word Deuteronomy means "second law," not because God gave a new law, but because Moses repeated and expounded the law for a new generation. The first generation redeemed from Egypt had died in the wilderness because of unbelief. Now their children stood at the border of the Promised Land, and Moses—an old man near the end of his life—preached a series of sermons reminding them of God's covenant, His commands, and His promises.

Deuteronomy is both deeply theological and deeply pastoral. It is a father's final charge to his children, urging them to love God fully and obey Him wholeheartedly. As we study this book, remember: what God wanted from Israel is still what He desires from us—our hearts, our love, and our obedience.

## Structure of Deuteronomy

1. Historical Review (Ch. 1–4)
    ◦ Moses recounts Israel's journey from Sinai to Moab.
    ◦ Lessons from past failures are recalled.
2. Exposition of the Law (Ch. 5–26)
    ◦ Repetition of the Ten Commandments (Ch. 5).
    ◦ The Shema: "Love the Lord your God" (Ch. 6).

- Laws for worship, leadership, justice, and social life.
3. Covenant Renewal (Ch. 27–30)
    - Blessings for obedience, curses for disobedience.
    - A choice between life and death, blessing and curse.
4. Final Words of Moses (Ch. 31–34)
    - Moses commissions Joshua.
    - Moses' song and blessing.
    - Moses' death on Mount Nebo.

## Key Themes of Deuteronomy

1. Love and Obedience – God desires a relationship based on love, expressed in obedience (Deut. 6:5).
2. Covenant Renewal – Each generation must personally embrace God's covenant.
3. God's Word – Life depends on hearing and obeying God's Word (Deut. 8:3).
4. Blessing and Curse – Obedience brings blessing, disobedience brings judgment.
5. Leadership – God promises a coming Prophet like Moses (Deut. 18:15).

## Exposition and Lessons

### 1. Remembering God's Works (Ch. 1–4)

Moses begins by reminding Israel of their history. He recalls their rebellion at Kadesh-Barnea, their wanderings, and their victories over Sihon and Og. He wants them to remember: God is faithful even when His people are not.

Lesson: We must learn from past failures, not repeat them. Memory is a spiritual discipline—forgetting God's works leads to unbelief.

## 2. Loving God with All Your Heart (Ch. 5–11)

Here Moses repeats the Ten Commandments and then gives the great Shema: "Hear, O Israel: The LORD our God, the LORD is one. Love the LORD your God with all your heart and with all your soul and with all your strength" (Deut. 6:4–5).

This is the heart of Deuteronomy. God wants more than rituals; He wants love. Teaching is emphasized: "These words... shall be on your heart. Teach them diligently to your children" (Deut. 6:6–7).

Lesson: True obedience flows from love. The greatest commandment is to love God fully, and from that love flows obedience and teaching the next generation.

## 3. Worship and Holiness (Ch. 12–16)

God commands centralization of worship, rejection of idols, and celebration of festivals (Passover, Weeks, Tabernacles). These ensured that Israel's identity remained rooted in God's covenant.

Lesson: Worship must be God-centered, not self-centered. Festivals reminded Israel (and us) that joy comes from remembering God's salvation.

## 4. Leadership and Justice (Ch. 17–20)

Moses gives laws concerning kings, priests, and prophets. Most striking is the prophecy of a future Prophet like Moses (Deut. 18:15): "The LORD your God will raise up for you a prophet like me... you shall listen to him." This points to Jesus, the ultimate Prophet and final Word of God (Acts 3:22).

Lesson: God provides leadership for His people, but ultimately points us to Christ, the true King, Priest, and Prophet.

## 5. Covenant Blessings and Curses (Ch. 27–30)

On Mounts Gerizim and Ebal, Israel was to declare blessings for obedience and curses for disobedience. Moses makes it clear: life and death are set before them. "I have set before you life and death, blessings and curses. Now choose life, so that you and your children may live" (Deut. 30:19).

Lesson: Obedience is not optional; it determines destiny. Every generation must make the choice.

## 6. The Death of Moses (Ch. 31–34)

Moses commissions Joshua, sings a prophetic song, blesses the tribes, and climbs Mount Nebo, where he sees the Promised Land but does not enter. He dies there, and God Himself buries him (Deut. 34:5–6).

Lesson: Even the greatest servant of God cannot fulfill the promise. A greater deliverer is needed—Jesus Christ.

### Christ in Deuteronomy

- The Prophet like Moses (18:15) – fulfilled in Jesus (Acts 3:22).
- The Word of God – Jesus resisted Satan with three quotes from Deuteronomy (Matt. 4:1–11).
- The Law on the Heart – anticipates the New Covenant (Jer. 31:33) fulfilled in Christ.
- Blessing and Curse – Christ became a curse for us (Gal. 3:13) so that we may receive God's blessing.

### Memory Verse

Deuteronomy 6:5 – "Love the LORD your God with all your heart and with all your soul and with all your strength."

## Reflection Questions

1. Why is remembering God's past works so important for faith today?
2. How does the Shema (Deut. 6:4–5) shape our understanding of obedience?
3. What do the blessings and curses teach us about the seriousness of covenant relationship?
4. How does Deuteronomy prepare the way for Jesus as the Prophet like Moses?
5. What does it mean to "choose life" in Christ today?

## Final Exhortation

Students, Deuteronomy is Moses' farewell sermon, but it is also God's timeless call to His people. It reminds us that faith is not inherited—it must be embraced personally. Every generation must hear, remember, love, and obey.

As you study this book, let Moses' words echo in your soul: "Choose life." Life is not found in idols, in disobedience, or in wandering hearts—it is found in loving God with all that you are.

Christ has fulfilled the law for us, taken the curse upon Himself, and given us His Spirit to write God's Word on our hearts. Now the call remains: will you love Him with all your heart, soul, and strength?

# { 6 }

# Joshua

The book of Joshua begins a new chapter in Israel's story. Moses, the great lawgiver, has died, and Joshua, his faithful servant, is now God's appointed leader. The wilderness wanderings are over; the time has come to inherit the land promised to Abraham, Isaac, and Jacob.

Joshua is a book of conquest and fulfillment. God's promises, made centuries earlier, are now realized. But this is not merely about Israel taking land—it is about God's faithfulness to His covenant and the call for His people to live courageously in obedience.

As you read Joshua, remember this: what God promises, He fulfills. Yet His promises also require our faith, courage, and obedience.

### Structure of Joshua

1. Entering the Land (Ch. 1–5)
   - Joshua commissioned as leader.
   - Crossing the Jordan.
   - The covenant renewed at Gilgal.
2. Conquering the Land (Ch. 6–12)
   - Jericho, Ai, southern and northern campaigns.
   - List of defeated kings.
3. Dividing the Land (Ch. 13–21)
   - Tribal allotments.
   - Cities of refuge.

- Levitical towns.
4. Serving the Lord in the Land (Ch. 22–24)
    - Eastern tribes return home.
    - Joshua's farewell addresses.
    - Covenant renewed at Shechem: "As for me and my house, we will serve the LORD."

### Key Themes of Joshua

1. God's Faithfulness: God fulfills every promise He made to the fathers (Joshua 21:45).
2. Courage and Obedience: "Be strong and courageous" (Joshua 1:9). Victory is tied to obedience.
3. Holiness of God: Sin cannot be tolerated in God's people (Achan's sin in Joshua 7).
4. Covenant Renewal: The people must continually recommit themselves to the Lord.
5. Rest in the Land: The Promised Land points forward to our rest in Christ (Hebrews 4).

### Exposition and Lessons

#### 1. Joshua Commissioned (Ch. 1)

God tells Joshua three times: "Be strong and courageous." Strength and courage are not found in self-confidence but in God's presence: "Do not be afraid... for the LORD your God is with you wherever you go" (1:9).

Lesson: True leadership flows from God's presence and God's Word. Success is defined by obedience, not military strategy.

## 2. Crossing the Jordan (Ch. 3–4)

As the priests carrying the Ark step into the Jordan, the waters part, and Israel crosses on dry ground—just as at the Red Sea. Twelve stones are set up as a memorial.

Lesson: God goes before His people. Every new generation must remember His power and pass that testimony on.

## 3. The Conquest Begins (Ch. 6–12)

- Jericho (Ch. 6): The walls fall, not by human strength but by obedience to God's unusual command.
- Ai (Ch. 7–8): Israel is defeated because of Achan's hidden sin. Once the sin is judged, victory comes.
- Southern and Northern Campaigns: God gives victory after victory, proving that no enemy can stand against His people when they obey.

Lesson: Victory comes not by might but by faith and obedience. Sin in the camp brings defeat.

## 4. Division of the Land (Ch. 13–21)

Though less dramatic, this section emphasizes God's faithfulness. Every tribe receives an inheritance. Cities of refuge are established for justice and mercy.

Lesson: God provides for all His people. His promises are specific and fulfilled in detail.

## 5. Covenant Renewal (Ch. 23–24)

In his farewell, Joshua warns against idolatry and compromise. He challenges Israel: "Choose this day whom you will serve... But as for me and my house, we will serve the LORD" (24:15).

Lesson: Every generation must decide whom they will serve. Faith cannot be borrowed—it must be personal.

## Key Lessons from Joshua

1. God's promises never fail—He fulfills every word.
2. Courage is required to walk in God's promises.
3. Sin must be dealt with seriously.
4. Every generation must renew its covenant with God.
5. The land was God's gift, but obedience was required to enjoy it.

## Christ in Joshua

- Joshua's Name: "Yehoshua" means "The LORD saves," the same root as "Jesus." Joshua points us to Christ, who leads His people into the true Promised Land.
- The Commander of the Lord's Army (5:13–15): Many believe this is a pre-incarnate appearance of Christ, leading His people into battle.
- Rest in the Land: Joshua gave Israel rest, but not ultimate rest (Hebrews 4:8–9). That rest comes only in Christ.

## Memory Verse

Joshua 1:9 – "Have I not commanded you? Be strong and courageous. Do not be afraid; do not be discouraged, for the LORD your God will be with you wherever you go."

## Reflection Questions

1. What does God's command "be strong and courageous" teach us about leadership and faith?

2. How does the crossing of the Jordan mirror the Red Sea, and why is this important for a new generation?
3. What lessons do we learn from Achan's sin at Ai?
4. Why was it important for Joshua to renew the covenant before his death?
5. How does Joshua point us forward to Jesus Christ?

## Final Exhortation

Students, Joshua teaches us that the God who promises is the God who fulfills. But it also reminds us that His promises require faith and obedience. Israel's victories came not by their swords but by God's power. Their defeats came when they ignored His holiness.

As you study this book, hear Joshua's challenge as your own: "Choose this day whom you will serve." The world offers many idols, but only the Lord is worthy of our service. May we, like Joshua, declare with confidence: "As for me and my house, we will serve the LORD."

# { 7 }

# Judges

If Joshua was a book of victory, then Judges is a book of decline. The generation that entered the land under Joshua saw God's mighty works, but the generation after them "did not know the LORD or the work that He had done for Israel" (Judges 2:10). As a result, Israel entered into a dark period of repeated failure.

Judges is a book of cycles—sin, oppression, crying out, deliverance, and then sin again. It is a tragic story, but also a hopeful one, for in every failure we see God's mercy. Judges shows us both the depth of human rebellion and the patience of God.

## Structure of Judges

1. Introduction: Israel's Failure (Ch. 1–2)
   - Partial conquest of the land.
   - Israel's unfaithfulness after Joshua's death
2. Cycles of Judges (Ch. 3–16)
   - A series of judges raised up by God: Othniel, Ehud, Deborah, Gideon, Jephthah, Samson, and others.
   - Each cycle follows the pattern:
     1. Israel sins.
     2. God sends oppression.
     3. Israel cries out.
     4. God raises a deliverer (judge).
     5. The land has peace—until the cycle repeats.

3. Epilogue: Israel's Corruption (Ch. 17–21)
   ◦ Stories of idolatry, immorality, civil war.
   ◦ The repeated refrain: "In those days there was no king in Israel; everyone did what was right in his own eyes."

## Key Themes of Judges

1. The Sin Cycle: Sin leads to slavery, but God delivers when His people repent.
2. The Need for Godly Leadership: Without a faithful leader, the people wander into chaos.
3. God's Mercy: Though His people fail repeatedly, God never abandons them.
4. Human Weakness vs. God's Power: God often uses the weak (Gideon, Deborah, Samson) to accomplish His will.
5. Pointing to a King: The book prepares the way for Israel's longing for a righteous king.

## Exposition and Lessons

### 1. Israel's Compromise (Ch. 1–2)

Instead of fully driving out the Canaanites, Israel compromised, leaving pockets of idolatry in the land. This disobedience sowed seeds of future corruption. Judges 2:19 sums it up: "Whenever the judge died, they turned back and were more corrupt than their fathers."

Lesson: Partial obedience is disobedience. What we tolerate today may enslave us tomorrow.

### 2. The First Judges (Ch. 3–5)

- Othniel: A model judge, faithful and effective.
- Ehud: A left-handed deliverer who killed the Moabite king.

- Deborah: A prophetess and judge who led Israel to victory alongside Barak.

Lesson: God raises leaders in unexpected ways—male or female, strong or weak—His Spirit empowers them.

### 3. Gideon: From Fear to Faith (Ch. 6–8)

Gideon begins fearful, hiding from the Midianites. God calls him "mighty warrior" before he sees himself that way. With only 300 men, Gideon defeats the Midianite army. Yet later he falls into idolatry with an ephod, showing even deliverers are flawed.

Lesson: God uses weak vessels, but pride and compromise can undo great victories.

### 4. Jephthah: Rash Vows (Ch. 11)

Jephthah, an outcast, is raised up to deliver Israel. But he makes a foolish vow, promising to sacrifice the first thing that comes from his house if God gives victory. Tragically, it is his daughter.

Lesson: God desires obedience, not rash promises. Leaders must be careful with their words.

### 5. Samson: Wasted Potential (Ch. 13–16)

Samson was set apart as a Nazarite from birth, blessed with supernatural strength. Yet his weakness for women led to repeated failures. Though he killed many Philistines, his life was marked by compromise. In the end, blind and humbled, he prayed, "O Lord God, remember me" (16:28), and God granted him one final act of deliverance.

Lesson: Gifts without holiness lead to destruction. God's mercy can redeem even a wasted life, but disobedience carries consequences.

## 6. *The Depths of Corruption (Ch. 17–21)*

The final chapters show Israel in moral chaos—idolatry, immorality, civil war. The refrain explains it all: "There was no king... everyone did what was right in his own eyes."

Lesson: Without God's rule, human hearts descend into chaos. Israel needed a true king, and so do we.

### Key Lessons from Judges

1. Sin always leads to bondage.
2. God is merciful even when His people fail.
3. Leadership matters—without godly leadership, people drift.
4. God uses the weak to shame the strong.
5. Every man doing what is "right in his own eyes" leads to destruction.

### Christ in Judges

- The Deliverers (Judges): Each judge points to the need for a greater Deliverer.
- Gideon's weakness, Samson's strength, Deborah's leadership—all foreshadow Christ as the perfect Judge.
- The refrain "no king in Israel" points to Christ, the Righteous King, who rules in justice and truth.

Judges teaches us that human saviors are temporary and flawed. We need the eternal Savior—Jesus Christ.

### Memory Verse

Judges 21:25 – "In those days there was no king in Israel; everyone did what was right in his own eyes."

## Reflection Questions

1. Why is the cycle of sin, oppression, and deliverance repeated so often in Judges?
2. What lessons do we learn from Gideon's faith and failures?
3. How does Samson's life warn us about wasting God's gifts?
4. Why is leadership so crucial for God's people?
5. How does Judges prepare us for the coming of Jesus as King?

## Final Exhortation

Students, Judges is a warning about what happens when God's people forget Him. It is also a testimony of God's mercy. Israel failed again and again, yet God raised up deliverers. But no judge could bring lasting peace. The book cries out for a true King—a King who will not die, who will not fail, who will not compromise.

That King is Jesus Christ. He is the Deliverer who breaks the cycle of sin once for all. He is the Righteous King who rules not by human opinion but by God's eternal truth.

As you study Judges, ask yourself: am I living by what is right in my own eyes, or by what is right in God's eyes? Only one path leads to life.

# { 8 }

# Ruth

After the dark cycles of sin, oppression, and rebellion in the book of Judges, we come to a beautiful story of light and redemption. The book of Ruth is like a sunrise after a long night. It shows us that even in the darkest times, God is at work, weaving His purposes through ordinary people and everyday events.

Ruth is not about kings or prophets, but about a widow, her daughter-in-law, and a faithful man in Bethlehem. Yet through their story, God reveals His providence, His covenant love, and His plan of redemption that ultimately leads to Christ.

## Background of Ruth

- Author: Unknown (traditionally Samuel).
- Date: Written during or after the time of the judges (1200–1000 BC).
- Setting: During the days of the judges, marked by famine and instability.
- Purpose: To show God's providence, the value of covenant loyalty, and the lineage leading to King David.

## Structure of Ruth

1. Ruth's Loyalty (Ch. 1)
    ◦ Naomi loses her husband and sons in Moab.

- Ruth chooses to stay with Naomi: "Your people shall be my people, and your God my God."
2. Ruth's Service (Ch. 2)
     - Ruth gleans in Boaz's field.
     - Boaz shows kindness and protection.
3. Ruth's Proposal (Ch. 3)
     - Naomi instructs Ruth to approach Boaz as a kinsman-redeemer.
     - Boaz agrees, but acknowledges another relative has first right.
4. Ruth's Redemption (Ch. 4)
     - Boaz redeems Ruth, marries her, and they have a son, Obed.
     - Obed becomes the grandfather of King David.

## Key Themes of Ruth

1. God's Providence – God works through "ordinary" events to accomplish extraordinary purposes.
2. Loyalty and Love – Ruth's devotion to Naomi models covenant faithfulness.
3. Redemption – Boaz as the kinsman-redeemer points to Christ.
4. Inclusion of the Nations – Ruth, a Moabite, is welcomed into God's people, foreshadowing the inclusion of Gentiles.
5. Hope in Dark Times – Even in the period of Judges, God is preparing for David—and ultimately for Jesus.

## Exposition and Lessons

### 1. Ruth's Loyalty (Ch. 1)

Naomi leaves Bethlehem for Moab due to famine. Tragedy strikes—her husband and sons die, leaving Naomi bitter and empty. Yet Ruth, her Moabite daughter-in-law, clings to her. Ruth's famous words (1:16) express total commitment: "Where you go I will go... your people will be my people, and your God my God."

Lesson: True faith is not convenience but covenant loyalty. Ruth's devotion mirrors God's loyal love (hesed).

### 2. Ruth's Service (Ch. 2)

In Bethlehem, Ruth gleans behind harvesters, gathering leftovers for survival. By God's providence, she ends up in the field of Boaz, a wealthy, godly relative. Boaz notices Ruth, protects her, and provides generously.

Lesson: God's providence is not usually seen in miracles but in "co-incidences" guided by His hand.

### 3. Ruth's Proposal (Ch. 3)

Naomi instructs Ruth to approach Boaz as a potential "kinsman-redeemer"—a relative responsible to redeem property and continue a family line. Ruth humbly requests: "Spread the corner of your garment over me, since you are a kinsman-redeemer."

Boaz commends her virtue and agrees, but first ensures legal order.

Lesson: Redemption is rooted in law but fulfilled in love.

### 4. Ruth's Redemption (Ch. 4)

At the city gate, Boaz legally redeems Naomi's land and marries Ruth. Their son, Obed, becomes part of the lineage of David, and ultimately of Christ (Matthew 1:5).

Lesson: God weaves personal redemption into His greater plan of salvation.

## Key Lessons from Ruth

1. God is at work even when life feels bitter. Naomi thought she returned empty, but God was writing a greater story.
2. Loyalty and faithfulness matter—Ruth's devotion reflects God's covenant love.
3. God's providence works through ordinary choices and circumstances.
4. Redemption requires a redeemer willing to pay the price. Boaz prefigures Christ, our Redeemer.
5. God's plan includes outsiders—Ruth the Moabite is grafted into the line of Christ.

## Christ in Ruth

- Boaz the Redeemer: Points to Christ, who redeems us from sin and makes us His bride.
- Ruth the outsider: Foreshadows the Gentiles brought into God's covenant family through Christ.
- The Line to David: Ruth's son Obed leads to David, and ultimately to Christ, the Son of David.

Ruth shows us redemption not only for one family but for the nations.

## Memory Verse

Ruth 1:16 – "Where you go I will go, and where you stay I will stay. Your people will be my people and your God my God."

## Reflection Questions

1. How does Ruth's loyalty to Naomi reflect true covenant love?

2. What does Ruth's story teach us about God's providence in everyday life?

3. How is Boaz's role as kinsman-redeemer fulfilled in Jesus Christ?

4. Why is it significant that Ruth, a Moabite, becomes part of Christ's genealogy?

5. What encouragement does Ruth's story give us in times of difficulty or loss?

## Final Exhortation

Students, Ruth reminds us that God is always at work, even in the darkest of times. While Judges shows us the chaos of rebellion, Ruth shows us the beauty of redemption. God uses ordinary people—widows, farmers, foreigners—to accomplish His extraordinary plan.

Never underestimate the providence of God in your life. That "chance meeting," that "unexpected turn"—it may be God positioning you for His purposes. And never forget: Christ is our Redeemer, who willingly paid the price to bring us into His family.

So, when life feels bitter, remember Naomi's story. When you feel like an outsider, remember Ruth's story. And when you need redemption, look to Jesus—the true Boaz, our Redeemer and King.

## { 9 }

# 1 Samuel

The book of 1 Samuel marks a turning point in Israel's history. Up to now, Israel was a loose confederation of tribes led by judges. But in 1 Samuel, the people cry out for a king, and the monarchy begins.

This book is not merely political history—it is spiritual history. It shows us the contrast between two kinds of leadership: Saul, the king chosen by the people's desire, and David, the king chosen by God's heart. Along the way, we meet Samuel, one of the greatest prophets, who serves as the bridge between the period of the judges and the kings.

1 Samuel reminds us that leadership matters. Leaders can either lead people into obedience or drag them into disobedience. But above all, it shows us that God is sovereign over history—He raises up leaders and brings them down according to His purpose.

### Background of 1 Samuel

- Author: Traditionally Samuel, with later prophets adding material.
- Date: Around 1100–1000 BC.
- Setting: Transition from judges to monarchy.
- Theme: God is sovereign and looks at the heart, not outward appearances.

## Structure of 1 Samuel

1. The Life of Samuel (Ch. 1–7)
    - Hannah's prayer and Samuel's birth.
    - Samuel's call as prophet.
    - Israel's victory under Samuel's leadership.
2. The Reign of Saul (Ch. 8–15)
    - Israel demands a king.
    - Saul chosen and anointed.
    - Saul's early victories.
    - Saul's disobedience and rejection.
3. The Rise of David (Ch. 16–31)
    - David anointed by Samuel.
    - David and Goliath.
    - Saul's jealousy and pursuit of David.
    - David spares Saul's life twice.
    - Saul's tragic end at Mount Gilboa.

## Key Themes of 1 Samuel

1. God's Sovereignty – God raises up and removes leaders.
2. Prayer – Hannah's prayer and Samuel's intercession show prayer's power.
3. The Danger of Disobedience – Saul loses his kingdom because he disobeyed.
4. The Heart Matters – God looks at the heart, not outward appearance (16:7).
5. Christ the True King – David points us to the greater Son of David, Jesus.

## Exposition and Lessons

### 1. Samuel's Birth and Call (Ch. 1–3)

Hannah, barren and mocked, prays earnestly for a son. God hears and gives her Samuel, whom she dedicates to the Lord. Samuel grows up in the tabernacle, and God calls him as prophet: "Speak, LORD, for your servant hears" (3:9).

Lesson: Prayer moves the hand of God, and God delights to raise up servants through humble beginnings.

### 2. Israel Demands a King (Ch. 8)

The people cry out: "Appoint for us a king... like all the nations" (8:5). Their desire reveals a lack of trust in God as King. God grants their request but warns them that a king will take, tax, and enslave.

Lesson: Be careful what you ask for. Sometimes God allows our desires to teach us that His will is better.

### 3. Saul's Rise and Fall (Ch. 9–15)

Saul begins well—tall, handsome, victorious in battle. But quickly he disobeys: offering unauthorized sacrifice (Ch. 13) and sparing what God commanded to destroy (Ch. 15). Samuel declares: "To obey is better than sacrifice" (15:22).

Lesson: Outward appearances impress people, but obedience impresses God.

### 4. David's Anointing and Victory (Ch. 16–18)

God sends Samuel to anoint David, the youngest son of Jesse. While Saul looked the part, David had the heart. Soon after, David faces Goliath, declaring: "The battle is the LORD's" (17:47). His faith triumphs where Saul's fear failed.

Lesson: God uses faith, not size or strength, to bring victory.

### 5. Saul's Jealousy and David's Trials (Ch. 19–26)

David becomes Saul's musician and armor-bearer, but Saul grows jealous of David's popularity. Twice David spares Saul's life, showing that true leadership waits on God's timing.

Lesson: Trust God's timing—do not seize what He has not yet given.

### 6. Saul's Tragic End (Ch. 28–31)

Saul, abandoned by God after persistent disobedience, consults a medium at Endor. He dies in battle on Mount Gilboa, a tragic end to a wasted opportunity.

Lesson: Disobedience hardens the heart. Saul's life warns us that leadership without submission to God leads to ruin.

## Key Lessons from 1 Samuel

1. God answers prayer and raises up leaders (Hannah and Samuel).
2. Leadership without obedience ends in failure (Saul).
3. God looks at the heart, not appearances (David).
4. Faith overcomes fear (David vs. Goliath).
5. God's timing must be trusted (David spares Saul).

## Christ in 1 Samuel

- Samuel as prophet, priest, and judge foreshadows Christ, who perfectly fulfills all three roles.
- David as the anointed king points to Jesus, the Son of David, the true King of kings.

- The rejection of Saul points to the rejection of human kingship in favor of God's chosen Messiah.

## Memory Verse

1 Samuel 16:7 – "For the LORD sees not as man sees: man looks on the outward appearance, but the LORD looks on the heart."

## Reflection Questions

1. What does Hannah's prayer teach us about faith and God's response?
2. Why did Israel's desire for a king reveal a lack of trust in God?
3. How does Saul's downfall warn us about partial obedience?
4. What can we learn from David's victory over Goliath?
5. How does David's patience with Saul teach us about waiting on God's timing?

## Final Exhortation

Students, 1 Samuel reminds us that God is sovereign in history and that leadership is a sacred trust. Saul teaches us the danger of pride and disobedience, while David shows us the power of faith and a heart after God.

But remember: even David was flawed. His reign points us to the greater Son of David, Jesus Christ, the perfect King who rules with justice, humility, and righteousness. As you read 1 Samuel, do not only see the rise of David—see the coming of Christ, the King of kings.

# { 10 }

# 2 Samuel

## (Expository Study)

My beloved students,

In 1 Samuel we saw the rise of David, the shepherd boy anointed to be king. In 2 Samuel, David takes the throne, unites the nation, and establishes Jerusalem as Israel's capital. Yet this book is not simply about David's triumphs—it is also about his failures.

2 Samuel presents David in all his humanity: a man after God's heart, yet capable of grievous sin. Through David's victories and defeats, we learn about God's covenant faithfulness, His mercy in forgiveness, and His justice in discipline. Above all, 2 Samuel points us to the greater Son of David—Jesus Christ—who would reign with perfect righteousness.

### Background of 2 Samuel

- Author: Traditionally Samuel (until his death), with prophets Nathan and Gad likely continuing.
- Date: Events around 1010–970 BC.

• Theme: God establishes His covenant with David and demonstrates mercy and justice through His dealings with David's reign.

## Structure of 2 Samuel

1. David's Rise to the Throne (Ch. 1–10)
     ◦ David laments Saul and Jonathan.
     ◦ David becomes king of Judah, then all Israel.
     ◦ Jerusalem becomes the capital.
     ◦ Ark of the Covenant brought to Jerusalem.
     ◦ God's covenant with David (Ch. 7).
     ◦ Military victories.
2. David's Sin and Its Consequences (Ch. 11–20)
     ◦ David and Bathsheba.
     ◦ Nathan confronts David.
     ◦ Absalom's rebellion.
     ◦ Civil unrest.
3. Appendix: David's Legacy (Ch. 21–24)
     ◦ Final acts of judgment and mercy.
     ◦ David's song of deliverance.
     ◦ David's mighty men.
     ◦ David's census and God's mercy.

## Key Themes of 2 Samuel

1. God's Covenant with David – God promises David an eternal throne (Ch. 7).
2. Sin Has Consequences – David's sin with Bathsheba brings lasting pain.
3. Repentance and Forgiveness – David models confession and reliance on God's mercy.

4. Leadership Under Pressure – David's reign reveals both the strengths and weaknesses of leadership.
5. Christ the True King – The promises to David are fulfilled in Christ.

## Exposition and Lessons

### 1. David's Rise and the Covenant (Ch. 1–10)

After Saul's death, David mourns deeply. Unlike Saul, David does not rejoice in his enemy's downfall but laments. He becomes king first in Hebron, then over all Israel. He captures Jerusalem and makes it the capital, bringing the Ark there with rejoicing (Ch. 6).

The pinnacle of these chapters is God's covenant with David (Ch. 7). God promises David an eternal house, kingdom, and throne. This covenant becomes central to the Old Testament, pointing to Christ as the Son of David who reigns forever (Luke 1:32–33).

Lesson: True greatness is found not in human ambition but in God's covenant promises.

### 2. David's Sin with Bathsheba (Ch. 11–12)

In one of the most sobering stories in Scripture, David, at the height of his power, falls into sin. He takes Bathsheba, the wife of Uriah, and arranges Uriah's death to cover it up. God sends Nathan to confront him with the parable of the ewe lamb. David confesses, "I have sinned against the LORD" (12:13).

Though forgiven, David faces consequences: family turmoil, rebellion, and grief.

Lesson: Even great leaders can fall. Sin always has consequences, but repentance brings forgiveness.

### 3. Family Rebellion and Civil War (Ch. 13–20)

David's household becomes a place of conflict. Amnon violates Tamar. Absalom murders Amnon and later leads a rebellion against David. Though David loves Absalom, the rebellion ends with Absalom's tragic death. David weeps: "O my son Absalom, my son, my son Absalom! Would I had died instead of you" (18:33).

Lesson: Sin spreads destruction, often beginning in the home. Yet even in discipline, God remains faithful to His covenant.

### 4. David's Legacy and Final Acts (Ch. 21–24)

The book closes with David's psalm of thanksgiving, his list of mighty men, and the account of his sinful census. God's judgment comes, but mercy is extended at the threshing floor of Araunah, where David offers sacrifice. That site becomes the future location of the temple.

Lesson: God's mercy triumphs over judgment, pointing us to Christ's ultimate sacrifice.

### Key Lessons from 2 Samuel

1. God exalts the humble and fulfills His covenant promises.
2. Sin, even forgiven, leaves scars—leadership carries great responsibility.
3. True repentance is marked by confession and turning back to God.
4. God's mercy triumphs over judgment.
5. The covenant with David points to Christ, the eternal King.

### Christ in 2 Samuel

- The Davidic Covenant (Ch. 7): Fulfilled in Christ, the Son of David, whose throne is eternal.

- David's Role as Shepherd-King: Foreshadows Christ, the Good Shepherd and King of kings.
- David's Mercy to Mephibosheth (Ch. 9): Reflects Christ's kindness to the undeserving.
- David's Intercession (Ch. 24): Points to Christ's ultimate intercession and sacrifice.

## Memory Verse

2 Samuel 7:16 – "Your house and your kingdom shall be made sure forever before me. Your throne shall be established forever."

## Reflection Questions

1. Why is the Davidic Covenant so central to understanding the Old Testament?
2. What does David's sin with Bathsheba teach us about temptation and consequences?
3. How does David's repentance in Psalm 51 model true confession?
4. What lessons can leaders learn from David's failures and successes?
5. How does 2 Samuel point us to Jesus as the true Son of David?

## Final Exhortation

Students, 2 Samuel is both inspiring and sobering. It inspires us with God's faithfulness to His covenant promises, and it sobers us with the reminder that even God's chosen servants are flawed. David's reign points us to a greater King, one without sin, who rules with justice and mercy.

When you study 2 Samuel, see both the faithfulness of David and the failures of David. But lift your eyes beyond David to Jesus, the

Son of David, whose throne is eternal. He is the King we long for, the King who never fails, the King who brings true peace.

# 1 Kings

The book of 1 Kings begins with great promise and ends with deep tragedy. It opens with the glory of Solomon's reign, the building of the magnificent temple, and the splendor of a united kingdom. But it closes with a divided kingdom, idolatry, and the seeds of destruction.

This book reminds us that leadership is a double-edged sword: godly leadership brings blessing, but ungodly leadership brings ruin. At its core, 1 Kings shows us that prosperity without faithfulness leads only to decline.

## Background of 1 Kings

- Author: Unknown, possibly compiled by prophets such as Jeremiah.
- Date: Covers events from ~970–850 BC.
- Theme: God blesses obedience and judges disobedience, especially in leadership.
- Key Verse: "As for you, if you walk before me faithfully with integrity of heart... I will establish your royal throne over Israel forever." (1 Kings 9:4–5)

## Structure of 1 Kings

1. The Reign of Solomon (Ch. 1–11)

- ◦ Solomon crowned king.
- ◦ Wisdom granted by God.
- ◦ Temple and palace built.
- ◦ Visit of the Queen of Sheba.
- ◦ Solomon's downfall into idolatry.

2. The Division of the Kingdom (Ch. 12)
   - ◦ Rehoboam's harshness.
   - ◦ Jeroboam's golden calves.
   - ◦ Israel divided into north (Israel) and south (Judah).

3. The Kings of Israel and Judah (Ch. 13–22)
   - ◦ Northern kings mostly wicked.
   - ◦ Rise of the prophet Elijah.
   - ◦ Conflict with Ahab and Jezebel.
   - ◦ Elijah on Mount Carmel.
   - ◦ Wars with Aram.

## Key Themes of 1 Kings

1. Wisdom and Foolishness – Solomon shows the heights of wisdom and the depths of folly.
2. Faithfulness vs. Idolatry – The kings are measured by their obedience to God.
3. The Role of the Prophets – Elijah demonstrates God's power against false gods.
4. Division and Decline – Sin splits God's people and weakens them.
5. Christ the Greater King – Solomon points to Christ, but fails; only Jesus reigns in perfect wisdom.

## Exposition and Lessons

### 1. Solomon Crowned King (Ch. 1–2)

David appoints Solomon as king. Solomon begins humbly, asking God for wisdom instead of wealth or power. God grants him unparalleled wisdom.

Lesson: True leadership begins with humility and dependence on God.

### 2. Solomon's Wisdom and Glory (Ch. 3–10)

Solomon's wisdom is displayed in the judgment of the two mothers (Ch. 3). His kingdom prospers, the temple is built, and nations admire Israel's greatness. The Queen of Sheba marvels at Solomon's wisdom and wealth.

Lesson: God blesses those who seek Him first. Wisdom is more valuable than riches.

### 3. Solomon's Downfall (Ch. 11)

Despite his wisdom, Solomon's many wives lead him into idolatry. His heart turns from the Lord, and God declares that the kingdom will be torn from his descendants.

Lesson: Great beginnings do not guarantee faithful endings. Compromise with sin leads to downfall.

### 4. Division of the Kingdom (Ch. 12)

Rehoboam, Solomon's son, refuses wise counsel and increases the people's burdens. Jeroboam leads the northern tribes to break away, forming the kingdom of Israel. He sets up golden calves in Bethel and Dan, leading Israel into sin.

Lesson: Pride and idolatry divide God's people.

### 5. *The Prophetic Ministry of Elijah (Ch. 17–19)*

Elijah bursts onto the scene, confronting King Ahab and Queen Jezebel. He declares drought, raises the widow's son, and calls down fire on Mount Carmel, proving that the LORD is God. Yet after victory, Elijah flees in fear, and God ministers to him gently.

Lesson: God's power is unmatched, yet His servants are human and need encouragement. God works not only in fire and wind but also in a gentle whisper.

### 6. *Ahab's Folly and God's Judgment (Ch. 20–22)*

King Ahab covets Naboth's vineyard and allows Jezebel to murder him for it. The prophet Elijah pronounces judgment: Ahab's house will fall. In battle, Ahab is killed, fulfilling God's word.

Lesson: God's justice cannot be avoided. Leaders are accountable for their actions.

## Key Lessons from 1 Kings

1. Wisdom without obedience leads to ruin.
2. Idolatry is the root of national and personal decline.
3. Division comes when leaders ignore God's Word.
4. Prophets remind us that God's voice is above kings.
5. God's justice is certain, but His mercy is available to the repentant.

## Christ in 1 Kings

- Solomon points to Christ as the true King of wisdom, yet fails to remain faithful.
- The Temple points to Christ, the true dwelling place of God among men (John 2:21).

- Elijah foreshadows John the Baptist, preparing the way for Christ.
- The Kingdom Divided reminds us of the unity Christ restores in His church.

## Memory Verse

1 Kings 18:21 – "How long will you waver between two opinions? If the LORD is God, follow Him; but if Baal is God, follow him."

## Reflection Questions

1. What lessons can we learn from Solomon's rise and fall?
2. How does idolatry still tempt God's people today?
3. Why was Elijah's confrontation on Mount Carmel so significant?
4. How does God's gentle whisper to Elijah encourage us in our weakness?
5. How does 1 Kings point us to Jesus as the greater King?

## Final Exhortation

Students, 1 Kings is both a book of glory and warning. Solomon's wisdom, wealth, and temple show us the heights of blessing when God is honored. But Solomon's idolatry and the kingdom's division show us the tragedy of turning from God.

Elijah's story reminds us that even in times of national apostasy, God raises faithful witnesses. And ultimately, this book makes us long for a King greater than Solomon—Jesus Christ, the One who reigns in perfect wisdom, righteousness, and justice.

Choose today whom you will follow. The question Elijah asked still echoes: "If the LORD is God, follow Him."

## { 12 }

# 2 Kings

The book of 2 Kings is one of the most sobering in the Old Testament. It continues the story from 1 Kings, beginning with the prophetic ministry of Elijah and Elisha, and ending with the tragic fall of both Israel (the northern kingdom) and Judah (the southern kingdom).

If 1 Kings was a story of decline, 2 Kings shows us the devastating consequences of persistent sin. Yet even here, God's mercy shines through: He raises up prophets to call His people back, and He preserves a faithful remnant. Above all, the book reminds us that God's Word is certain—His promises of blessing and warnings of judgment both come to pass.

### Background of 2 Kings

- Author: Unknown, possibly a prophetic historian (tradition associates it with Jeremiah).
- Date: Covers events from ~850–586 BC.
- Theme: God's Word is sure—obedience brings blessing, disobedience brings judgment.
- Key Verse: "The LORD warned Israel and Judah by every prophet and every seer... but they would not listen." (2 Kings 17:13–14)

## Structure of 2 Kings

1. The Ministry of Elisha (Ch. 1–10)
    - Elijah taken to heaven.
    - Elisha's miracles and prophetic ministry.
    - Jehu's purge of Ahab's house.
2. The Decline and Fall of Israel (Ch. 11–17)
    - Wicked kings rule the north.
    - Assyrian conquest of Samaria (722 BC).
3. The Decline and Fall of Judah (Ch. 18–25)
    - Hezekiah's reforms.
    - Manasseh's wickedness.
    - Josiah's revival.
    - Babylon conquers Jerusalem (586 BC).

## Key Themes of 2 Kings

1. God's Word Always Comes True – Prophets declare both blessings and curses, and history confirms them.
2. God's Patience and Judgment – God warns repeatedly, but judgment comes when warnings are ignored.
3. Leadership Shapes a Nation – Kings influence the people toward either faithfulness or rebellion.
4. Prophetic Ministry – Prophets like Elisha speak truth to power and display God's power.
5. Hope Beyond Exile – Though the nation falls, God's promises to David and His people remain.

## Exposition and Lessons

### 1. Elijah's Departure and Elisha's Ministry (Ch. 1–10)

The book opens with Elijah taken to heaven in a whirlwind, a chariot of fire carrying him away. His mantle falls to Elisha, who continues his ministry with even greater miracles: purifying water, multiplying oil, raising the dead, healing Naaman the leper, and blinding enemy armies.

Lesson: God's work continues through new servants. His power is not bound to one man.

### 2. *The Fall of the Northern Kingdom (Ch. 11–17)*

Israel continues in idolatry under kings like Jehu, Jeroboam II, and Hoshea. Despite prophetic warnings, the people persist in sin. Finally, Assyria invades, and Samaria falls in 722 BC. The people are exiled, fulfilling God's warnings.

The Bible is clear about why: "This happened because the people of Israel had sinned against the LORD their God" (17:7).

Lesson: Persistent sin without repentance brings judgment.

### 3. *Hezekiah's Faith and Deliverance (Ch. 18–20)*

In Judah, Hezekiah stands out as a righteous king. When Assyria threatens Jerusalem, he seeks the Lord. God sends an angel who destroys 185,000 Assyrian soldiers in one night. Later, when Hezekiah falls ill, God extends his life by 15 years.

Lesson: Prayer moves God's hand. Faith in God's power delivers His people.

### 4. *Manasseh's Wickedness (Ch. 21)*

Hezekiah's son Manasseh becomes Judah's most wicked king, filling Jerusalem with idolatry and bloodshed. His sins seal Judah's fate. Though later humbled, his reign demonstrates how one leader can corrupt a nation.

Lesson: Sin tolerated at the top spreads throughout the nation.

### 5. Josiah's Revival (Ch. 22–23)

Josiah becomes king as a boy and leads a great revival. When the Book of the Law is rediscovered, he tears his clothes in repentance. He renews the covenant, destroys idols, and restores true worship.

Lesson: God's Word brings revival. A single leader's devotion can transform a nation, though temporarily.

### 6. The Fall of Jerusalem (Ch. 24–25)

Despite Josiah's reforms, Judah returns to sin. Babylon invades under Nebuchadnezzar, destroying Jerusalem and the temple in 586 BC. The people are taken into exile. Yet even here, hope remains: the book ends with Jehoiachin, a Davidic king, shown mercy in Babylon—a small reminder that God's covenant with David is not forgotten.

Lesson: God disciplines His people, but He does not abandon His promises.

## Key Lessons from 2 Kings

1. God's Word is certain—His warnings and promises both come true.
2. Prophets are God's messengers of truth in dark times.
3. Leadership has lasting consequences for good or evil.
4. Prayer and faith bring deliverance, even against impossible odds.
5. God's judgment is real, but His covenant love endures beyond exile.

## Christ in 2 Kings

- Elisha's miracles foreshadow Christ's works of healing and provision.

- Hezekiah's deliverance points to Christ's ultimate victory over enemies.
- Josiah's revival anticipates Christ's cleansing of the temple.
- The exile prepares for Christ, who brings restoration and a new covenant.
- Jehoiachin's release points to God's faithfulness to David's line, ultimately fulfilled in Jesus.

## Memory Verse

2 Kings 17:13 – "The LORD warned Israel and Judah through all His prophets and seers: 'Turn from your evil ways. Obey my commands and decrees.'"

## Reflection Questions

1. What do Elijah's departure and Elisha's ministry teach us about God's ongoing work?
2. Why did Israel fall to Assyria, and what lessons can we learn about sin's consequences?
3. How does Hezekiah's faith encourage us when facing overwhelming challenges?
4. What does Josiah's revival teach us about the power of God's Word?
5. How does the end of 2 Kings point us to hope in Christ?

## Final Exhortation

Students, 2 Kings is a heavy book, filled with warnings about the dangers of sin and disobedience. Yet it also shines with hope. Elisha's miracles remind us of God's compassion, Hezekiah's prayers show us God's power, and Josiah's revival reveals the transforming strength of God's Word.

The fall of Israel and Judah was not the end—it was discipline to prepare God's people for a greater King. Jesus Christ, the Son of David, came not to rebuild a temple of stone but to build a kingdom of redeemed hearts.

When you study 2 Kings, let it remind you that God's Word is sure. Judgment is real, but so is grace. Sin brings exile, but Christ brings us home.

## { 13 }

# 1 Chronicles

The book of 1 Chronicles may at first seem difficult, beginning with nine chapters of genealogies. Yet behind those long lists of names lies a profound truth: God remembers His people. Every name matters to Him. Every generation is connected in His plan.

While 1 and 2 Samuel and Kings emphasize the political and moral history of Israel, Chronicles retells the story with a spiritual focus. The writer (traditionally Ezra) wanted the returning exiles to remember their roots, their worship, and their covenant identity. Thus, 1 Chronicles highlights the reign of David—not his failures, but his role in preparing for the temple and leading God's people in worship.

If Samuel and Kings show us Israel's failures, Chronicles shows us God's faithfulness.

### Background of 1 Chronicles

- Author: Jewish tradition attributes it to Ezra.
- Date: Written after the exile (~450–400 BC).
- Audience: Returning exiles who needed hope and a reminder of their spiritual heritage.
- Theme: God's people must center their lives on worship and covenant faithfulness.
- Key Verse: "If my people, who are called by my name, will humble themselves and pray... then I will hear from heaven and

forgive their sin and heal their land." (2 Chronicles 7:14, but reflects the spirit of Chronicles).

## Structure of 1 Chronicles

1. Genealogies (Ch. 1–9)
     - From Adam to post-exilic generations.
     - Emphasis on the tribes of Judah and Levi.
2. The Reign of David (Ch. 10–29)
     - Saul's death (Ch. 10).
     - David's rise and mighty men.
     - The Ark brought to Jerusalem.
     - David's psalms of worship.
     - Preparations for the temple.
     - David's final instructions to Solomon.

## Key Themes of 1 Chronicles

1. God's Covenant Faithfulness – God's promises to David and Israel endure beyond exile.
2. The Centrality of Worship – The Ark, the temple, the priests, and the Levites are emphasized.
3. The Role of Leadership – David leads not just politically but spiritually.
4. God's People Remembered – The genealogies remind us of God's care for every generation.
5. Hope After Exile – God is not finished with His people; their story continues.

## Exposition and Lessons

### 1. The Genealogies (Ch. 1–9)

The opening chapters trace history from Adam through Abraham, Israel, and David. To modern readers, this may feel tedious. But for Israel, just returning from exile, it was deeply encouraging. Their identity was not lost—God had preserved them.

Lesson: God remembers every name. No life is forgotten in His plan.

### 2. Saul's Death and David's Rise (Ch. 10–12)

Saul's death is briefly mentioned, paving the way for David. The Chronicler highlights David's mighty men and the tribes who rallied to him, showing God's hand in establishing his reign.

Lesson: Leadership is confirmed by God's calling and the unity of His people.

### 3. The Ark Brought to Jerusalem (Ch. 13–16)

David desires to bring the Ark to Jerusalem, but at first does so incorrectly, resulting in Uzzah's death. Later, following God's instructions, the Ark is brought with great joy and worship. David organizes choirs, musicians, and priests to continually give thanks.

Lesson: Worship must be according to God's Word, not human ideas. True worship is joyful, reverent, and constant.

### 4. God's Covenant with David (Ch. 17)

God promises David that his dynasty will endure forever and that his son will build the temple. David responds with humility: "Who am I, O LORD God, and what is my family, that you have brought me this far?" (17:16).

Lesson: God's covenant is by grace, not human merit. Gratitude should always be our response.

### 5. David's Reign and Preparations (Ch. 18–27)

David's military victories are described, but the emphasis is on his preparations for the temple. He gathers materials, organizes the Levites, and arranges musicians and gatekeepers. Though he cannot build the temple, he devotes his life to preparing for it.

Lesson: Even if we do not see the completion of God's work in our lifetime, we can prepare the way for others.

### 6. David's Final Instructions (Ch. 28–29)

In his old age, David commissions Solomon: "Be strong and courageous, and do the work. Do not be afraid or discouraged, for the LORD God... is with you" (28:20). David leads the people in joyful giving for the temple. The book ends with David's death and Solomon's succession.

Lesson: A leader's final legacy is not wealth or power but faithfulness in pointing others to God.

### Key Lessons from 1 Chronicles

1. God remembers His people and keeps His promises.
2. Worship must be central in the life of God's people.
3. Leadership should inspire unity, worship, and preparation for God's work.
4. God's covenant is by grace; our response must be gratitude.
5. Preparing the way for future generations is a mark of true leadership.

## Christ in 1 Chronicles

- The Davidic Covenant points to Christ, the eternal Son of David.
- The Temple Preparations point to Christ, the true temple where God dwells with His people.
- David's Kingship foreshadows Christ's perfect rule.
- The Genealogies emphasize God's faithfulness in preserving the line that leads to Jesus.

## Memory Verse

1 Chronicles 28:20 – "Be strong and courageous, and do the work. Do not be afraid or discouraged, for the LORD God, my God, is with you."

## Reflection Questions

1. Why are the genealogies important for Israel—and for us today?
2. What lessons do we learn from David's desire to bring the Ark to Jerusalem?
3. How does the covenant with David strengthen our faith in God's promises?
4. Why was worship so central to David's reign?
5. How does 1 Chronicles point us to Christ as the eternal King?

## Final Exhortation

Students, 1 Chronicles reminds us that God remembers His people and His promises. Even after exile, even after failure, God was still faithful. David's reign, seen through the lens of worship and covenant, points us to Christ, the Son of David, who builds a greater temple—the church—and reigns forever.

Do not despise the "genealogies" in your own life—the seasons or details that seem insignificant. God is writing a story through every name, every generation, every moment. And like David, may our lives be marked by worship, gratitude, and preparation for the glory of God.

## { 14 }

# 2 Chronicles

The book of 2 Chronicles continues the story of God's people with a distinct focus: the reign of Solomon, the temple, and the kings of Judah. Unlike Kings, which presents both the northern and southern kingdoms, Chronicles concentrates on Judah, the line of David, and especially on the central role of worship in the temple.

The Chronicler (traditionally Ezra) wrote for the returning exiles, reminding them that their survival as a nation depended not on military might or political power, but on faithfulness to the covenant and worship of the one true God. This message is still vital for us today: revival and blessing come when God's people humble themselves, pray, seek His face, and turn from their wicked ways.

### Background of 2 Chronicles

- Author: Jewish tradition attributes it to Ezra.
- Date: ~450–400 BC, after the exile.
- Audience: The Jewish remnant restored to the land.
- Theme: God blesses those who seek Him and disciplines those who forsake Him.
- Key Verse: "If my people, who are called by my name, will humble themselves and pray and seek my face and turn from their wicked ways, then I will hear from heaven, and I will forgive their sin and will heal their land." (2 Chronicles 7:14)

## Structure of 2 Chronicles

1. The Reign of Solomon (Ch. 1–9)
   - Solomon's wisdom.
   - Construction and dedication of the temple.
   - Solomon's wealth and fame.
2. The Kings of Judah (Ch. 10–36)
   - Division of the kingdom (focus on Judah).
   - Reigns of Asa, Jehoshaphat, Joash, Hezekiah, Josiah, and others.
   - Repeated pattern: when the king seeks God, blessing follows; when he forsakes God, judgment comes.
   - Ends with the Babylonian exile and Cyrus' decree to return.
3. The Centrality of Worship – The temple is at the heart of Israel's life with God.
4. The Power of Prayer – God hears and responds to His people when they seek Him.
5. The Example of Leadership – Kings set the spiritual tone of the nation.
6. Blessing and Judgment – Obedience brings prosperity, disobedience brings defeat.
7. Hope Beyond Exile – The story ends not with despair, but with the promise of return.

## Exposition and Lessons

### 1. Solomon's Reign (Ch. 1–9)

Solomon begins by asking God for wisdom, and God blesses him with wealth and honor as well. His greatest achievement is building the temple. The dedication in chapter 7 is marked by fire from heaven and God's glory filling the house. God promises to hear the prayers offered in this place.

Lesson: True wisdom begins with seeking God, and true greatness is measured by devotion to Him.

## 2. *The Pattern of the Kings (Ch. 10–36)*

The Chronicler carefully shows the pattern of Judah's kings:

- Asa sought God and found peace, but later relied on foreign alliances.
- Jehoshaphat trusted God in battle and saw victory through worship, but compromised with wicked alliances.
- Joash began well under the guidance of Jehoiada the priest but turned to idolatry later.
- Hezekiah brought great revival, restoring temple worship and celebrating Passover.
- Manasseh, Judah's most wicked king, humbled himself in captivity and was restored—a testimony to God's mercy.
- Josiah rediscovered the Book of the Law, led sweeping reforms, and renewed the covenant.
- Later kings forsook God, leading to Babylon's destruction of Jerusalem.

Lesson: The direction of a nation often follows the heart of its leaders. Seeking God brings blessing; forsaking Him brings ruin.

## 3. *The Fall and the Return (Ch. 36)*

The book ends with the exile to Babylon. Yet it does not close in despair. The final verses recount the decree of Cyrus, king of Persia, inviting the Jews to return and rebuild the temple. Even in judgment, God provides hope.

Lesson: God's promises are not nullified by human failure. He disciplines, but He also restores.

## Key Lessons from 2 Chronicles

1. God responds to humble prayer and repentance (7:14).
2. Worship is central to the life of God's people.
3. Leadership has spiritual consequences for entire nations.
4. God's mercy is greater than our failures—repentance opens the door to restoration.
5. Even after judgment, God's plan of redemption continues.

## Christ in 2 Chronicles

- The Temple points to Christ, the true dwelling place of God among men.
- The Davidic Line continues through Judah, leading to Jesus, the Messiah.
- The Promise of Restoration anticipates Christ's greater restoration through the cross.
- The Kings point to our need for a perfect King—fulfilled only in Jesus.

## Memory Verse

2 Chronicles 7:14 – "If my people, who are called by my name, will humble themselves and pray and seek my face and turn from their wicked ways, then I will hear from heaven, and I will forgive their sin and will heal their land."

## Reflection Questions

1. Why was the temple so important to Israel's identity and worship?
2. How does the pattern of Judah's kings illustrate the consequences of seeking or forsaking God?
3. What does the story of Manasseh teach us about God's mercy?

4. Why is 2 Chronicles 7:14 such a key verse for God's people in every generation?

5. How does the conclusion of 2 Chronicles give hope to people living after failure?

## Final Exhortation

Students, 2 Chronicles reminds us that worship is central, prayer is powerful, and leadership matters. It shows us the blessings of revival and the consequences of rebellion. Yet even when God's people fail, His mercy is greater.

The returning exiles who first read this book needed to know that God had not abandoned them. And we need the same assurance today. In Christ, the true Temple and the eternal King, we find restoration and hope.

So, humble yourself, pray, and seek His face. For the God of 2 Chronicles is the same today—faithful to forgive, mighty to restore, and worthy of all worship.

## { 15 }

# Ezra

The book of Ezra is a story of new beginnings. After seventy years of exile in Babylon, God fulfills His promise and brings His people back to the land. The temple that had been destroyed is rebuilt, worship is restored, and God's law is once again at the center of Israel's life.

Ezra reminds us that God is faithful to His Word, even when His people have failed. It also teaches us that true revival is not just about buildings but about hearts—hearts humbled before God's Word and dedicated to His holiness.

### Background of Ezra

- Author: Traditionally Ezra, a priest and scribe.
- Date: Covers events from ~538–458 BC.
- Audience: Jews returning from Babylonian exile.
- Theme: God restores His people through His Word, worship, and covenant faithfulness.
- Key Verse: "For Ezra had set his heart to study the Law of the LORD, and to do it and to teach His statutes and rules in Israel." (Ezra 7:10)

### Structure of Ezra

1. The First Return under Zerubbabel (Ch. 1–6)

- Cyrus' decree to return.
- Rebuilding of the altar and temple foundation.
- Opposition and delay.
- Temple completed and dedicated.

2. The Second Return under Ezra (Ch. 7–10)
- Ezra's journey to Jerusalem.
- Ezra's devotion to God's Word.
- Confronting sin and intermarriage.
- Covenant renewal.

## Key Themes of Ezra

1. God's Faithfulness – He fulfills His promise to bring His people back from exile.
2. The Power of God's Word – Ezra's devotion to Scripture brings spiritual renewal.
3. Worship Restored – The temple and sacrifices are central again.
4. Holiness – God's people must separate from sin to be His holy people.
5. Leadership and Reform – Faithful leaders guide God's people back to covenant faithfulness.

## Exposition and Lessons

### 1. The First Return (Ch. 1–6)

Cyrus, king of Persia, issues a decree allowing the Jews to return and rebuild the temple—fulfilling Jeremiah's prophecy. Zerubbabel leads about 50,000 back to Jerusalem. They rebuild the altar first, showing that worship is their priority.

Opposition from surrounding nations causes delays, but through the encouragement of the prophets Haggai and Zechariah, the temple is completed and dedicated with joy.

Lesson: God stirs the hearts of leaders and people to accomplish His purposes, despite opposition.

### 2. Ezra's Arrival (Ch. 7–8)

Decades later, Ezra the scribe arrives with a new group of exiles. The text highlights his devotion: "Ezra had set his heart to study the Law of the LORD, to do it, and to teach it" (7:10). Ezra embodies the model of a godly leader—devoted to God's Word in study, obedience, and teaching.

Lesson: True revival begins with God's Word. Leaders must first live it before they can teach it.

### 3. Confronting Sin (Ch. 9–10)

Ezra is devastated to learn that many of the people, including leaders, had intermarried with pagan nations, threatening their covenant identity. In deep grief and prayer, Ezra confesses the nation's sins before God. The people respond with repentance, separating from ungodly practices.

Lesson: Repentance is essential for renewal. Holiness means turning away from sin and back to God.

### Key Lessons from Ezra

1. God's promises never fail—He brings His people home.
2. Worship must be central in the life of God's people.
3. Revival begins with God's Word, studied, obeyed, and taught.
4. Opposition is inevitable, but God's purposes cannot be stopped.
5. Repentance and holiness are necessary for lasting renewal.

## Christ in Ezra

- The Return from Exile points to Christ, who brings ultimate restoration from sin's exile.
- The Temple points to Christ as the true temple (John 2:21).
- Ezra the Scribe foreshadows Christ, the Word made flesh, who teaches with authority.
- The Covenant Renewal anticipates Christ's New Covenant written on our hearts.

## Memory Verse

Ezra 7:10 – "For Ezra had set his heart to study the Law of the LORD, and to do it and to teach His statutes and rules in Israel."

## Reflection Questions

1. What does the rebuilding of the temple teach us about the priority of worship?
2. How did God use both kings (like Cyrus) and prophets (like Haggai and Zechariah) to accomplish His purposes?
3. Why is Ezra's devotion to God's Word such an important model for us today?
4. What does Ezra's response to sin teach us about repentance and holiness?
5. How does the book of Ezra point us to Christ as our ultimate restorer?

## Final Exhortation

Students, the book of Ezra is about more than stones and walls—it is about hearts and worship. God restored His people not only to their land but to Himself. He raised up leaders like Zerubbabel and

Ezra to remind them that His Word and His holiness must guide every step.

We, too, live as exiles in this world, waiting for the full restoration Christ will bring. Until then, we are called to live as a holy people, devoted to God's Word, centered in worship, and quick to repent when we fall short.

Take courage from Ezra's story: God keeps His promises, restores His people, and uses leaders who set their hearts on His Word. May you, like Ezra, be a student of the Word, a doer of the Word, and a teacher of the Word.

## { 16 }

# Nehemiah

The book of Nehemiah is a testimony to what God can do through a servant with a burdened heart, a clear vision, and unwavering faith. While Ezra focuses on rebuilding the temple and restoring worship, Nehemiah focuses on rebuilding the walls of Jerusalem and restoring the people's resolve to live as God's covenant people.

Walls were more than stone barriers—they symbolized identity, security, and separation from sin. Without walls, Jerusalem was vulnerable and incomplete. Nehemiah, a cupbearer to the king of Persia, left his position of comfort to lead God's people in this critical mission. His story offers us powerful lessons in leadership, prayer, perseverance, and holiness.

### Background of Nehemiah

- Author: Traditionally Nehemiah, later combined with Ezra as one book.
- Date: Mid-5th century BC (~445–432 BC).
- Setting: Jerusalem during Persian rule.
- Theme: God restores His people physically and spiritually through godly leadership.
- Key Verse: "The God of heaven will give us success. We His servants will start rebuilding." (Nehemiah 2:20)

## Structure of Nehemiah

1. Nehemiah's Burden and Mission (Ch. 1–2)
    ◦ Nehemiah's prayer.
    ◦ Permission from King Artaxerxes.
    ◦ Surveying Jerusalem's ruins.
2. Rebuilding the Walls (Ch. 3–7)
    ◦ Organizing the workers.
    ◦ Facing opposition.
    ◦ Completion of the wall in 52 days.
3. Revival through God's Word (Ch. 8–10)
    ◦ Ezra reads the Law publicly.
    ◦ People confess sins and renew covenant.
4. Reforms and Dedication (Ch. 11–13)
    ◦ Dedication of the wall with great joy.
    ◦ Nehemiah's reforms in worship, Sabbath, and holiness.

## Key Themes of Nehemiah

1. Prayerful Leadership – Every major step begins with prayer.
2. Vision and Perseverance – God uses focused leaders to accomplish great tasks.
3. Opposition and Resistance – God's work always faces opposition.
4. The Power of God's Word – Revival comes through Scripture.
5. Holiness and Separation – God's people must live distinct lives.

## Exposition and Lessons

### 1. Nehemiah's Burden (Ch. 1–2)

When Nehemiah hears that Jerusalem's walls are broken and its gates burned, he weeps, fasts, and prays. His prayer acknowledges sin and appeals to God's covenant mercy. God grants him favor with King Artaxerxes, who sends him to rebuild.

Lesson: True leadership begins with a burden and prayer. Before Nehemiah built walls, he bowed in prayer.

## 2. Rebuilding the Walls (Ch. 3–7)

Nehemiah organizes the people, each repairing a section of wall. Opposition comes from enemies like Sanballat and Tobiah, who mock, threaten, and scheme. Nehemiah responds with prayer, vigilance, and perseverance. In just 52 days, the walls are completed—a miracle of God's enabling.

Lesson: God's work requires unity, perseverance, and faith in the face of opposition.

## 3. Revival by the Word (Ch. 8–10)

After the wall is completed, the focus turns to spiritual renewal. Ezra reads the Law publicly, and the people weep as they hear it. Nehemiah reminds them: "The joy of the LORD is your strength" (8:10). Confession and covenant renewal follow.

Lesson: Physical rebuilding is meaningless without spiritual renewal. God's Word is central to revival.

## 4. Dedication and Reforms (Ch. 11–13)

The wall is dedicated with choirs and great rejoicing. But Nehemiah also institutes reforms—removing foreigners from temple service, restoring tithes, enforcing Sabbath observance, and opposing intermarriage with pagan nations. Nehemiah's closing prayer is repeated: "Remember me, O my God, for good."

Lesson: Holiness requires continual vigilance. Leaders must have the courage to confront sin.

## Key Lessons from Nehemiah

1. Prayer must saturate every step of God's work.
2. God calls leaders who are willing to sacrifice comfort for service.
3. Opposition is inevitable, but perseverance brings victory.
4. Revival comes through God's Word, not just external reform.
5. Holiness must be pursued continually, not just occasionally.

## Christ in Nehemiah

- Nehemiah the Builder points to Christ, the ultimate Builder of His church (Matthew 16:18).
- The Walls Restored symbolize the protection Christ provides for His people.
- The Covenant Renewal anticipates the New Covenant in Christ's blood.
- Nehemiah's Sacrifice reflects Christ, who left heaven's glory to restore His people.

## Memory Verse

Nehemiah 8:10 – "Do not grieve, for the joy of the LORD is your strength."

## Reflection Questions

1. What does Nehemiah's response to Jerusalem's broken walls teach us about leadership?
2. How can we apply Nehemiah's example of prayer and planning in our own lives?
3. Why is unity so important in accomplishing God's work?
4. What role did God's Word play in the revival of Nehemiah's day?

5. How does Nehemiah's story point us to Christ as the greater Builder and Restorer?

## Final Exhortation

Students, Nehemiah teaches us that rebuilding is not just about walls but about hearts. God used Nehemiah because he cared deeply, prayed earnestly, and led courageously. But Nehemiah also knew that lasting strength came not from stone walls but from the joy of the Lord.

In our lives, we may face broken walls—situations of vulnerability, discouragement, or defeat. Nehemiah's story reminds us that God can restore, rebuild, and renew. And it points us to Christ, who not only rebuilds walls but restores souls.

So, take courage. Pray first, work faithfully, endure opposition, and find your strength in the joy of the Lord. For He is the Builder and Keeper of His people.

# { 17 }

# Esther

The book of Esther is unique among the books of the Bible. It never once mentions the name of God, yet His hand is evident in every page. It is a story of providence, courage, and deliverance, showing us that even when God seems hidden, He is still at work behind the scenes for the good of His people.

Esther tells how a Jewish orphan girl became queen of Persia and, through her bravery and faith, was used by God to save her people from annihilation. This book reminds us that God's purposes cannot be thwarted, and that He often raises up ordinary people for extraordinary tasks.

### Background of Esther

- Author: Unknown (possibly Mordecai).
- Date: ~5th century BC, during Persian rule.
- Setting: Susa, the Persian capital.
- Theme: God preserves His people through His providence, even when He seems hidden.
- Key Verse: "And who knows whether you have not come to the kingdom for such a time as this?" (Esther 4:14)

### Structure of Esther

1. Esther Becomes Queen (Ch. 1–2)

- ○ Queen Vashti removed.
- ○ Esther chosen as queen.
2. Haman's Plot (Ch. 3–4)
    - ○ Haman plots to destroy the Jews.
    - ○ Mordecai urges Esther to intercede.
3. Esther's Courage (Ch. 5–7)
    - ○ Esther risks her life before the king.
    - ○ Haman's plot begins to unravel.
    - ○ Haman executed on his own gallows.
4. The Jews Delivered (Ch. 8–10)
    - ○ A new decree allows Jews to defend themselves.
    - ○ Great victory and joy.
    - ○ Feast of Purim established.

## Key Themes of Esther

1. God's Providence – Even when unseen, God directs events for His purposes.
2. Courage in Crisis – Esther risks her life to save her people.
3. The Reversal of Evil – God turns the schemes of the wicked against themselves.
4. The Preservation of God's People – God ensures His covenant people are not destroyed.
5. God Uses Ordinary People – Esther and Mordecai were not priests or prophets, yet God used them mightily.

## Exposition and Lessons

### 1. Esther Becomes Queen (Ch. 1–2)

When Queen Vashti refuses King Xerxes' command, she is deposed. Esther, a young Jewish woman raised by her cousin Mordecai, is chosen as queen. Though her heritage is hidden, God positions her for His purpose.

Lesson: God often places His people strategically, even when they don't see the bigger plan.

## 2. Haman's Plot (Ch. 3–4)

Haman, promoted in the Persian court, becomes enraged when Mordecai refuses to bow to him. He convinces the king to issue a decree to destroy all Jews. Mordecai urges Esther to intercede, telling her: "Who knows whether you have not come to the kingdom for such a time as this?"

Lesson: God raises us up for specific times and purposes. Courageous obedience may cost us, but it can change history.

## 3. Esther's Courage (Ch. 5–7)

Esther risks her life by approaching the king without being summoned—a crime punishable by death unless the king extends his scepter. She wisely invites the king and Haman to two banquets. At the second, she reveals Haman's plot against her people. Haman is executed on the very gallows he built for Mordecai.

Lesson: God turns evil plots into opportunities for deliverance. Faith often requires risking comfort and safety.

## 4. The Jews Delivered (Ch. 8–10)

Because Persian law could not be revoked, a new decree is issued allowing the Jews to defend themselves. On the appointed day, instead of being destroyed, the Jews triumph over their enemies. The feast of Purim is established to commemorate this deliverance.

Lesson: God's people may face great danger, but His providence ensures their ultimate survival.

## Key Lessons from Esther

1. God's providence is at work even when He seems silent.
2. Courage is required to fulfill God's calling.
3. The schemes of the wicked will ultimately fail.
4. God preserves His people to fulfill His promises.
5. Ordinary people in ordinary places can be used for extraordinary purposes.

## Christ in Esther

- Mordecai's Intercession foreshadows Christ, who intercedes for His people.
- Esther's Willingness to Risk Her Life points to Christ, who gave His life to save His people.
- The Great Reversal of Haman's plot points to the cross, where Satan's scheme was turned into God's victory.
- The Preservation of the Jews ensured the coming of Christ, the promised Messiah.

## Memory Verse

Esther 4:14 – "And who knows whether you have not come to the kingdom for such a time as this?"

## Reflection Questions

1. How does the book of Esther teach us about God's providence when He seems absent?
2. Why was Esther's courage so critical in God's plan of deliverance?
3. What does Haman's downfall teach us about pride and evil schemes?
4. How does the Feast of Purim remind us of God's faithfulness?

5. How does Esther point us to Christ, our ultimate Deliverer?

## Final Exhortation

Students, Esther teaches us that even when God seems silent, He is sovereign. His name may not be written in the text, but His fingerprints are all over the story. He raises up Esther, positions Mordecai, and turns Haman's evil into good.

This book challenges us: Are we willing to step into God's calling, even when it costs us? Like Esther, we may find ourselves in situations where silence is safer, but obedience is necessary. And like Esther, we must trust that God has placed us "for such a time as this."

Above all, Esther points us to Christ, who risked not just a throne but gave His life to save us. And in Him, we are assured that God's providence is still at work in our lives today.

# Job

The book of Job confronts one of life's hardest questions: Why do the righteous suffer? Job was a blameless man, yet he lost his wealth, health, and children in a series of devastating trials. His friends insisted he must have sinned, but Job maintained his innocence and cried out for answers.

Through Job's story, we learn that suffering is not always punishment. Sometimes it is a test of faith, a means of refining character, or a stage for God's glory. Most importantly, Job shows us that God's wisdom is greater than ours, and our role is not always to understand but to trust.

### Background of Job

- Author: Unknown (possibly the earliest written book of the Bible).
- Date: Patriarchal period (~2000 BC).
- Setting: The land of Uz.
- Theme: God is sovereign over suffering, and faith must rest in Him, not in circumstances.
- Key Verse: "Though he slay me, yet will I hope in him." (Job 13:15)

## Structure of Job

1. Prologue: Job Tested (Ch. 1–2)
   - Job's prosperity.
   - Satan's challenge.
   - Job's suffering begins.
2. Dialogues: Job and His Friends (Ch. 3–37)
   - Job's lament.
   - Three cycles of debates with Eliphaz, Bildad, and Zophar.
   - Elihu's speech.
3. God's Answer (Ch. 38–41)
   - God speaks from the whirlwind.
   - Declares His wisdom and power.
4. Epilogue: Job Restored (Ch. 42)
   - Job repents in humility.
   - God restores his fortunes.

## Key Themes of Job

1. The Mystery of Suffering – We may not always know the reason for suffering.
2. Faith Under Trial – True faith clings to God even without answers.
3. God's Sovereignty – God rules over creation and even over Satan.
4. The Limits of Human Wisdom – Job's friends misapplied truth, showing our need for divine wisdom.
5. Hope Beyond Suffering – God restores and vindicates the faithful.

## Exposition and Lessons

### 1. The Test of Job (Ch. 1–2)

Job is introduced as upright and blameless. Yet Satan challenges God, claiming Job only serves Him because of blessings. God allows Job to be tested—his wealth, children, and health are stripped away. Job's response: "The LORD gave, and the LORD has taken away; blessed be the name of the LORD" (1:21).

Lesson: Faith is proven genuine when it endures loss without turning from God.

### 2. The Debates (Ch. 3–37)

Job's friends argue that suffering is always the result of sin. They urge Job to repent, but Job insists he has not sinned in a way that explains his suffering. Their error was not in their theology (sin can bring suffering) but in misapplying it to Job's case.

Lesson: We must be careful not to judge others in their suffering. Sometimes silence and compassion are better than explanations.

### 3. Job's Cry for a Redeemer (Ch. 19)

Amid despair, Job declares a profound hope: "I know that my Redeemer lives, and that in the end he will stand on the earth" (19:25). This statement shines as a prophecy of Christ, our Redeemer, who gives hope beyond suffering.

Lesson: Even in pain, faith looks to the living Redeemer.

### 4. God's Answer (Ch. 38–41)

God does not explain Job's suffering but reveals His majesty in creation: the stars, seas, animals, and forces of nature all testify to

His wisdom and power. The message is clear: if Job cannot under-stand creation, how can he fully understand God's purposes?

Lesson: God's ways are higher than ours. Trust is better than ex-planation.

### 5. Job's Restoration (Ch. 42)

Job repents in humility: "I spoke of things I did not understand" (42:3). God restores his fortunes, doubling his wealth and blessing him with a new family. More importantly, Job's relationship with God is deepened through suffering.

Lesson: God honors faith that endures trial. Restoration may come in this life, but the ultimate restoration is eternal.

## Key Lessons from Job

1. Suffering is not always punishment; it may be a test or refining fire.
2. Friends should comfort, not condemn, the suffering.
3. Faith looks beyond circumstances to the living Redeemer.
4. God's wisdom surpasses human understanding.
5. Endurance in suffering leads to blessing and maturity.

## Christ in Job

- Job the Innocent Sufferer foreshadows Christ, who suffered though blameless.
- Job's Cry for a Mediator (9:33) points to Christ, our Mediator between God and man.
- The Redeemer Lives (19:25) directly points to Christ's resurrec-tion.
- God's Sovereignty in Job's Trials shows us the cross, where suf-fering accomplished redemption.

## Memory Verse

Job 19:25 – "I know that my Redeemer lives, and that in the end he will stand on the earth."

## Reflection Questions

1. What does Job's story teach us about the relationship between suffering and faith?
2. Why were Job's friends wrong in their approach to his suffering?
3. How does Job's cry for a Redeemer point us to Christ?
4. What lessons can we learn from God's response out of the whirlwind?
5. How does Job help us trust God in our own unanswered questions?

## Final Exhortation

Students, the book of Job is not meant to answer every question about suffering—it is meant to point us to God. Job's story reminds us that trials may come even to the faithful, but God's sovereignty and wisdom are greater than our pain.

When you suffer, remember: you may not understand, but you can trust. And like Job, you can declare with confidence: "I know that my Redeemer lives."

Christ is that Redeemer. He suffered though innocent, triumphed through resurrection, and now offers us hope that suffering will not have the final word.

# { 19 }

# Psalms

The book of Psalms is the hymnbook of the Bible. It gives voice to the full range of human experience—joy and sorrow, faith and doubt, praise and lament. When we cannot find the words to pray, the Psalms provide them.

This collection of 150 songs and prayers, written over centuries by David, Asaph, the sons of Korah, Moses, Solomon, and others, teaches us how to worship with honesty and reverence. The Psalms remind us that God desires not polished performances but hearts poured out before Him.

Above all, the Psalms point us to Christ—the ultimate King, Shepherd, and Redeemer—who fulfills their deepest hopes.

### Background of Psalms

- Authors: Multiple (David wrote ~73; Asaph, sons of Korah, Moses, Solomon, and others contributed).
- Date: ~1400–400 BC.
- Setting: From wilderness wanderings to temple worship in Jerusalem.
- Theme: Honest worship of God in every season of life.
- Key Verse: "Let everything that has breath praise the LORD." (Psalm 150:6)

## Structure of Psalms

The Psalms are divided into five books, mirroring the five books of Moses:

1. Book I (Ps. 1–41) – David's personal prayers, laments, and praises.
2. Book II (Ps. 42–72) – Corporate worship and cries for deliverance.
3. Book III (Ps. 73–89) – National laments and God's covenant faithfulness.
4. Book IV (Ps. 90–106) – God's reign and Israel's history.
5. Book V (Ps. 107–150) – Songs of thanksgiving, trust, and final doxology.

## Key Themes of Psalms

1. Worship in Every Circumstance – Praise and lament both honor God.
2. God's Kingship – He reigns over nations and history.
3. Messianic Hope – Many psalms point forward to Christ.
4. The Power of Prayer – God invites honest cries from His people.
5. The Joy of God's Presence – God is our refuge, shepherd, and salvation.

## Exposition and Lessons

### 1. Psalms of Lament

Nearly half of the Psalms are laments, expressing grief, fear, or confusion. For example, "How long, O LORD? Will you forget me forever?" (Ps. 13:1). Yet even in lament, the psalmists return to trust: "But I trust in your unfailing love" (13:5).

Lesson: Faith is not the absence of questions but the decision to trust God in the midst of them.

## 2. Psalms of Praise and Thanksgiving

These celebrate God's greatness and goodness: "The LORD is my shepherd; I shall not want" (Ps. 23:1). Thanksgiving psalms (like Ps. 100) call all creation to worship.

Lesson: Praise shifts our focus from our problems to God's power.

## 3. Messianic Psalms

Several psalms point directly to Christ:

- Psalm 2 – The Messiah as King.
- Psalm 22 – The suffering Savior ("My God, my God, why have you forsaken me?").
- Psalm 110 – The priest-king fulfilled in Jesus.

Lesson: The Psalms give us prophetic glimpses of Christ's suffering, reign, and priesthood.

## 4. Wisdom Psalms

Some psalms (like Ps. 1 and Ps. 119) emphasize living by God's Word. Psalm 119, the longest chapter in the Bible, exalts Scripture as our guide and delight.

Lesson: True blessing comes from meditating on God's Word day and night.

## 5. *Psalms of Trust*

These psalms express confidence in God's care: "God is our refuge and strength, an ever-present help in trouble" (Ps. 46:1).

Lesson: Trust is the anchor of worship—it steadies us through storms.

### Key Lessons from Psalms

1. God invites us to bring every emotion before Him.
2. Worship is not limited to joy; lament can also glorify God.
3. The Psalms teach us how to pray, praise, and trust.
4. God's Word is a source of life and guidance.
5. The Psalms prepare us for Christ, the ultimate King and Savior.

### Christ in Psalms

- The Suffering Servant in Psalm 22 foreshadows Christ's crucifixion.
- The Good Shepherd in Psalm 23 points to Christ (John 10:11).
- The Reigning King in Psalm 2 and 110 reveals Christ's authority.
- The Cornerstone in Psalm 118 points to Christ as the foundation of salvation.
- The Word of God exalted in Psalm 119 finds fulfillment in Christ, the Living Word.

### Memory Verse

Psalm 100:4 – "Enter his gates with thanksgiving and his courts with praise; give thanks to him and praise his name."

## Reflection Questions

1. Why are both lament and praise important parts of worship?
2. How do the Psalms teach us to pray more honestly before God?
3. Which psalms most clearly point us to Christ, and how?
4. How does Psalm 119 describe the role of God's Word in our lives?
5. What role should the Psalms play in our daily worship and devotion?

## Final Exhortation

Students, the book of Psalms is a treasure chest of worship and prayer. It teaches us that we can come to God with joy or sorrow, thanksgiving or complaint—and He welcomes it all. The Psalms invite us into raw honesty with God, while also lifting our eyes to His greatness.

Above all, the Psalms point us to Christ—the Shepherd who walks with us, the King who reigns, the Suffering Servant who redeems, and the Living Word who guides us.

So let us, with the psalmist, "bless the LORD at all times; His praise shall continually be in my mouth" (Ps. 34:1).

{ 20 }

# Proverbs

The book of Proverbs is God's textbook on wisdom. While Psalms teaches us how to pray and worship, Proverbs teaches us how to live. Its short sayings and vivid instructions guide us in relationships, work, speech, money, morality, and character.

Written largely by Solomon—the wisest man of his day—Proverbs reminds us that wisdom is not just intelligence but skillful living rooted in the fear of the Lord. It is practical, down-to-earth, and timeless. And in Christ, we discover the fulfillment of Proverbs, for He is the wisdom of God (1 Cor. 1:30).

## Background of Proverbs

- Author: Primarily Solomon, with contributions from Agur, Lemuel, and other wise men.
- Date: ~10th century BC (during Solomon's reign).
- Purpose: To impart wisdom for godly living.
- Theme: The fear of the Lord is the beginning of wisdom.
- Key Verse: "The fear of the LORD is the beginning of knowledge, but fools despise wisdom and instruction." (Proverbs 1:7)

## Structure of Proverbs

1. Prologue: The Call of Wisdom (Ch. 1–9)
   ◦ Contrast of wisdom and folly.

- Wisdom personified as a woman calling out.
  - Admonitions from father to son.
2. Solomon's Proverbs (Ch. 10–22:16)
   - Short, practical sayings about daily life.
3. Sayings of the Wise (Ch. 22:17–24:34)
   - Additional teachings on discipline and integrity.
4. More Proverbs of Solomon (Ch. 25–29)
   - Collected during King Hezekiah's reign.
5. Sayings of Agur and Lemuel (Ch. 30–31)
   - Agur's humility and reflections.
   - Lemuel's mother's advice.
   - The virtuous woman (31:10–31).

## Key Themes of Proverbs

1. The Fear of the Lord – Reverence for God is the foundation of wisdom.
2. Wisdom vs. Folly – Life is a choice between two paths.
3. The Power of Words – Speech can bring life or destruction.
4. Work and Laziness – Diligence leads to blessing, laziness to poverty.
5. Relationships – Family, friends, and community shaped by wisdom.
6. Integrity and Character – True success comes from righteousness.

## Exposition and Lessons

### 1. The Fear of the Lord (Ch. 1–9)

Proverbs begins with the foundation: wisdom begins with fearing the Lord. This is not terror but reverence—recognizing God as holy, sovereign, and the source of all truth. Wisdom is portrayed as a woman calling out in the streets, inviting all to walk in her ways.

Lesson: True wisdom is not just intellectual but spiritual—it begins with God.

## 2. *Wisdom in Daily Life (Ch. 10–29)*

These chapters present hundreds of short sayings about real-life issues:

- Words – "A gentle answer turns away wrath, but a harsh word stirs up anger" (15:1).
- Work – "Go to the ant, you sluggard; consider its ways and be wise" (6:6).
- Wealth – "Honor the LORD with your wealth, with the first-fruits of all your crops" (3:9).
- Friendship – "A friend loves at all times, and a brother is born for adversity" (17:17).
- Discipline – "Whoever spares the rod hates their children, but the one who loves their children is careful to discipline them" (13:24).

Lesson: God cares about the details of everyday living—speech, work, money, and relationships.

## 3. *Wisdom for Leaders (Ch. 16–29)*

Several proverbs address kings and rulers, emphasizing justice, humility, and integrity. Leadership without wisdom leads to destruction, but leadership rooted in righteousness brings stability.

Lesson: Whether in government, business, or the church, leaders must seek wisdom from God.

## 4. *Words of Agur and Lemuel (Ch. 30–31)*

Agur humbly confesses his limitations but acknowledges God's wisdom. Lemuel's mother advises him against drunkenness, lust, and injustice, urging him to defend the rights of the poor.

Proverbs ends with the famous description of the virtuous woman—a picture of wisdom embodied in daily life: hardworking, generous, trustworthy, and God-fearing.

Lesson: True wisdom shapes not only great leaders but also faithful homes.

## Key Lessons from Proverbs

1. The fear of the Lord is the foundation for wise living.
2. Wisdom is practical, shaping speech, work, money, and relationships.
3. Words carry great power—use them for life, not destruction.
4. Laziness leads to ruin; diligence leads to blessing.
5. Godly character is more valuable than wealth or status.

## Christ in Proverbs

- Wisdom Personified in Proverbs 8 points to Christ, who is the wisdom of God (1 Cor. 1:24).
- The Righteous King anticipated in Proverbs finds fulfillment in Christ's perfect reign.
- The Virtuous Woman foreshadows the church, the bride of Christ, clothed with strength and dignity.
- Every Proverb fulfilled in Christ, who lived with perfect wisdom.

## Memory Verse

Proverbs 3:5–6 – "Trust in the LORD with all your heart and lean not on your own understanding; in all your ways submit to him, and he will make your paths straight."

## Reflection Questions

1. What does it mean to "fear the Lord," and why is it the foundation of wisdom?
2. How do the proverbs about speech challenge the way you use words?
3. Which proverb about work or diligence speaks most to your life right now?
4. How does the virtuous woman in Proverbs 31 inspire your view of wisdom in daily living?
5. How does Christ embody the wisdom of Proverbs?

## Final Exhortation

Students, Proverbs teaches us that wisdom is not abstract—it is practical. It is found not in lofty theories but in everyday choices: how we speak, work, treat others, and honor God. The fear of the Lord is its foundation, and Christ is its fulfillment.

Let the Proverbs be your daily companion. Read them, memorize them, and apply them. For wisdom is more precious than rubies, and nothing you desire can compare with her (Prov. 3:15).

# { 21 }

# Ecclesiastes

The book of Ecclesiastes is unlike any other in the Bible. It is raw, philosophical, and often unsettling. Attributed to Solomon, "the Preacher" (Qoheleth), it chronicles a man's search for meaning in life. Over and over, we hear the refrain: "Vanity of vanities! All is vanity" (1:2).

Ecclesiastes shows us the futility of life lived "under the sun"—that is, life lived apart from God. Wealth, pleasure, work, wisdom, and success all prove empty when pursued as ends in themselves. Yet, by the end of the book, the Preacher points us to the conclusion of the matter: "Fear God and keep his commandments, for this is the whole duty of man" (12:13).

## Background of Ecclesiastes

- Author: Traditionally Solomon (called "the Preacher" or Qoheleth).
- Date: ~10th century BC.
- Purpose: To show the emptiness of life without God and point to true meaning in Him.
- Theme: Life is meaningless without God, but purposeful when lived for Him.
- Key Verse: "Fear God and keep his commandments, for this is the whole duty of man." (Ecclesiastes 12:13)

## Structure of Ecclesiastes

1. The Vanity of Life (Ch. 1–2)
   ◦ The futility of wisdom, pleasure, and work.
2. The Seasons of Life (Ch. 3–5)
   ◦ A time for everything under heaven.
   ◦ Wealth and toil without God are meaningless.
3. Observations on Life (Ch. 6–8)
   ◦ The limitations of human wisdom.
   ◦ Injustice, oppression, and the brevity of life.
4. Wisdom for Living (Ch. 9–11)
   ◦ The uncertainty of life.
   ◦ Enjoy God's gifts with gratitude.
5. The Conclusion of the Matter (Ch. 12)
   ◦ Remember your Creator in youth.
   ◦ Fear God and keep His commandments.

## Key Themes of Ecclesiastes

1. The Vanity of Life Without God – All earthly pursuits are fleeting.
2. The Brevity of Life – Time passes quickly; death is inevitable.
3. The Fear of God – True meaning is found only in reverence and obedience to God.
4. The Gift of Enjoyment – Life's pleasures are good when received from God's hand.
5. Wisdom's Limits – Human understanding cannot grasp all of God's purposes.

## Exposition and Lessons

### 1. Life "Under the Sun" (Ch. 1–2)

The Preacher surveys wisdom, pleasure, wealth, and work, only to find them empty. He declares, "What does man gain by all the toil at which he toils under the sun?" (1:3). All achievements fade; nothing lasts.

Lesson: A life centered on self and the world will ultimately feel empty, no matter how successful.

### 2. A Time for Everything (Ch. 3)

Ecclesiastes 3 presents the famous poem: "For everything there is a season, and a time for every matter under heaven" (3:1). Life is full of cycles beyond our control. Yet God has placed eternity in our hearts (3:11), reminding us that we long for something beyond time.

Lesson: Contentment comes from trusting God's timing and recognizing our eternal purpose.

### 3. The Limits of Wealth and Work (Ch. 5–6)

The Preacher warns of the dangers of riches: "Whoever loves money never has money enough" (5:10). Wealth cannot satisfy, and toil without God is meaningless.

Lesson: True joy comes not from possessions but from receiving life as God's gift.

### 4. The Reality of Death (Ch. 7–9)

Both the wise and the foolish die. This reality humbles us. The Preacher urges: "Go, eat your bread with joy, and drink your wine with a merry heart, for God has already approved what you do" (9:7).

Lesson: Death is certain, but life's joys can be embraced when viewed as gifts from God.

### 5. Remember Your Creator (Ch. 12)

The book closes with a poetic picture of aging and death: the dimming eyes, trembling hands, and failing body. The conclusion is clear: "Fear God and keep his commandments, for this is the whole duty of man" (12:13).

Lesson: The key to life is not endless striving but humble obedience to God.

## Key Lessons from Ecclesiastes

1. Life without God is empty, no matter how successful it looks.
2. God has placed eternity in our hearts—we long for Him.
3. Contentment is found in trusting God's timing and gifts.
4. Death is inevitable; prepare by living for God now.
5. True meaning is found in fearing God and keeping His commands.

## Christ in Ecclesiastes

- The Emptiness "Under the Sun" points to our need for Christ, who brings eternal life.
- The Gift of Enjoyment is fulfilled in Christ, who gives abundant life (John 10:10).
- The Longing for Eternity is answered in Christ, who sets eternity in our hearts.
- The Conclusion to Fear God points to Christ, who enables us to live in obedience.

## Memory Verse

Ecclesiastes 12:13 – "Fear God and keep his commandments, for this is the whole duty of man."

## Reflection Question

1. Why does the Preacher call life "vanity"?
2. What does Ecclesiastes 3 teach us about God's sovereignty over time?
3. Why can't wealth and pleasure bring lasting satisfaction?
4. How does remembering our Creator in youth shape the rest of life?
5. How does Christ fulfill the longings expressed in Ecclesiastes?

## Final Exhortation

Students, Ecclesiastes is a sobering but liberating book. It shatters the illusions of self-made success and teaches us that apart from God, life is empty. But with Him, every breath, every task, every joy has meaning.

The Preacher's final conclusion is still true today: Fear God and keep His commandments. In Christ, we find not only the wisdom to live but the eternal purpose that makes life worth living.

So do not chase the wind. Instead, chase after God, for only He can satisfy the eternity He has placed within your heart.

# Song of Solomon

The Song of Solomon (also called the Song of Songs) is one of the most beautiful and misunderstood books in the Bible. At first glance, it seems to be a romantic love poem between a bride (the Shulammite woman) and her groom (often identified as Solomon). Yet throughout history, God's people have recognized it as more than human romance—it is a divine picture of love: both the beauty of marital love and the greater love of Christ for His people.

This book teaches us that love is God's gift—pure, powerful, and sacred. In a world that often distorts love and sexuality, Song of Solomon reminds us that true love is covenantal, faithful, and deeply fulfilling. At the same time, it points us to the ultimate Bridegroom, Jesus Christ, who loves His church with an everlasting love.

## Background of Song of Solomon

- Author: Traditionally Solomon (though some see it as a collection of love poems).
- Date: ~10th century BC.
- Theme: The beauty of covenant love, both human and divine.
- Key Verse: "Many waters cannot quench love; rivers cannot sweep it away." (Song of Solomon 8:7)

## Structure of Song of Solomon

1. The Bride and Groom's Love (Ch. 1–2)
    ◦ Expressions of affection.
    ◦ Desire for intimacy.
2. The Growth of Love (Ch. 3–5)
    ◦ Longing and separation.
    ◦ The wedding and union.
3. The Power of Love (Ch. 6–8)
    ◦ Celebration of marital delight.
    ◦ The strength and permanence of love.

## Key Themes of Song of Solomon

1. The Beauty of Marital Love – Love, intimacy, and romance are God's design.
2. The Exclusivity of Love – True love is faithful and covenantal.
3. The Power of Love – Love is strong, enduring, and unquenchable.
4. Christ and His Church – The love between bride and groom points to Christ's love for His people.
5. Purity and Passion – Godly love blends purity with passion in a holy way.

## Exposition and Lessons

### 1. Love's Delight (Ch. 1–2)

The book begins with passionate words: "Let him kiss me with the kisses of his mouth—for your love is more delightful than wine" (1:2). The bride delights in the groom, and he praises her beauty. Their love is mutual and joyful.

Lesson: God created love and intimacy to be celebrated within marriage.

## 2. Love's Longing (Ch. 3)

The bride dreams of searching for her beloved through the city streets until she finds him. This reflects the deep longing of love to be united and secure.

Lesson: True love desires commitment and closeness, not distance or detachment.

## 3. Love's Union (Ch. 4–5)

The wedding imagery appears as the groom describes the bride with poetic admiration. Their love is consummated in marital intimacy, celebrated without shame. Yet soon after, separation occurs, and the bride anxiously searches for her beloved again—showing the tension between closeness and distance in human relationships.

Lesson: Marriage is a journey with seasons of joy and challenges, but love perseveres.

## 4. Love's Power (Ch. 6–8)

The latter chapters overflow with praise, delight, and commitment. The climactic statement declares: "Many waters cannot quench love; rivers cannot sweep it away" (8:7). Love is stronger than trials, richer than wealth, and more enduring than life itself.

Lesson: True love is powerful and permanent because it is rooted in God.

### Key Lessons from Song of Solomon

1. Love and intimacy are God's good gifts, to be honored and enjoyed in marriage.
2. True love is covenantal, faithful, and exclusive.
3. Marital love reflects Christ's covenant love for His church.
4. Passion and purity belong together in God's design.

5. Love is enduring and unquenchable when rooted in God's covenant.

## Christ in Song of Solomon

- The Bridegroom points to Christ, who loves the church and gave Himself for her (Eph. 5:25).
- The Bride represents the church, longing for union with Christ.
- The Wedding Imagery anticipates the marriage supper of the Lamb (Rev. 19:7–9).
- The Strength of Love fulfilled in Christ's everlasting love, which death itself cannot quench.

## Memory Verse

Song of Solomon 8:7 – "Many waters cannot quench love; rivers cannot sweep it away."

## Reflection Questions

1. What does Song of Solomon teach us about God's design for love and marriage?
2. How can this book correct cultural distortions of love and intimacy?
3. In what ways does the bride's longing for her beloved picture our longing for Christ?
4. How does the permanence of love in 8:7 reflect Christ's love for His church?
5. How should we celebrate and protect the beauty of covenant love today?

## Final Exhortation

Students, the Song of Solomon is a holy reminder that love is God's gift. It is not something to be cheapened, distorted, or hidden—it is to be celebrated as a reflection of His covenant faithfulness.

In marriage, it teaches us to honor love's purity, passion, and permanence. In Christ, it points us to the greater reality: the Bridegroom who gave His life for His Bride, and who will one day welcome us to the marriage feast of the Lamb.

So whether you are single or married, let this book stir your heart toward deeper love—both human and divine. For many waters cannot quench love, and Christ's love for you endures forever.

## { 23 }

# Isaiah

The book of Isaiah is often called the "fifth Gospel" because of its vivid prophecies of Jesus Christ. Written over 700 years before Christ's birth, Isaiah proclaims both judgment on sin and the glorious promise of salvation through the coming Messiah.

Isaiah ministered during a time of political upheaval, when Judah was tempted to trust in alliances rather than in the Lord. Through his prophetic vision, Isaiah called God's people to repentance, warned of coming judgment, and promised hope in the Servant of the Lord who would bring salvation to all nations.

This book shows us the holiness of God, the seriousness of sin, and the greatness of Christ's saving work.

### Background of Isaiah

- Author: Isaiah, son of Amoz.
- Date: ~740–680 BC.
- Setting: Judah during the reigns of Uzziah, Jotham, Ahaz, and Hezekiah.
- Theme: God is holy and just, yet merciful; He offers salvation through the promised Messiah.
- Key Verse: "Though your sins are like scarlet, they shall be as white as snow." (Isaiah 1:18)

## Structure of Isaiah

1. Judgment on Judah and the Nations (Ch. 1–39)
     ◦ Call to repentance.
     ◦ Warnings of Assyrian invasion.
     ◦ God's sovereignty over the nations.
2. Comfort and Salvation (Ch. 40–66)
     ◦ The greatness of God.
     ◦ The Servant Songs.
     ◦ Promise of a new heaven and new earth.

## Key Themes of Isaiah

1. The Holiness of God – Isaiah's vision of God's holiness (Ch. 6).
2. Judgment on Sin – Both Judah and the nations are accountable.
3. The Remnant – God preserves a faithful people.
4. The Servant of the Lord – Prophecies of the suffering and exalted Messiah.
5. Salvation for the Nations – God's plan extends beyond Israel to all peoples.

## Exposition and Lessons

### 1. The Vision of God's Holiness (Ch. 6)

Isaiah sees the Lord seated on a throne, high and exalted, with seraphim crying, "Holy, holy, holy is the LORD Almighty" (6:3). Overwhelmed by his sin, Isaiah cries, "Woe is me!" But God cleanses him and commissions him.

Lesson: A true encounter with God's holiness leads to humility, cleansing, and mission.

## 2. Judgment on Judah and the Nations (Ch. 1–39)

Isaiah warns Judah that their empty worship and injustice will bring judgment. He declares that Assyria will be God's instrument of discipline. Yet he also assures them that God will preserve a faithful remnant and ultimately bring deliverance.

Lesson: God is just—He judges sin but preserves His people.

## 3. The Promise of Immanuel (Ch. 7)

In the face of political fear, Isaiah promises a miraculous sign: "The virgin will conceive and give birth to a son, and will call him Immanuel" (7:14). This prophecy points directly to the birth of Christ, God with us.

Lesson: Our hope in crisis is not human alliances but God's presence.

## 4. The Suffering Servant (Ch. 52–53)

Perhaps the most powerful prophecy of Christ in the Old Testament is Isaiah 53: "He was pierced for our transgressions, he was crushed for our iniquities." The Servant of the Lord suffers as a substitute for sinners, bearing our punishment and bringing us peace.

Lesson: Salvation is by substitution—Christ took our place on the cross.

## 5. The Glory of Salvation (Ch. 40–66)

These chapters overflow with comfort: "Comfort, comfort my people" (40:1). God promises forgiveness, restoration, and a new creation. Isaiah ends with the hope of new heavens and a new earth where righteousness dwells.

Lesson: God's salvation is not just for Israel but for all nations, and it culminates in eternal renewal.

## Key Lessons from Isaiah

1. God is holy, and sin cannot stand before Him.
2. God judges nations, but He also preserves a remnant.
3. Salvation comes through the Messiah, the Servant of the Lord.
4. God's promises point us to hope beyond judgment.
5. Christ fulfills Isaiah's vision of suffering, salvation, and glory.

## Christ in Isaiah

- Immanuel (7:14) – Fulfilled in Christ's virgin birth.
- Wonderful Counselor, Mighty God (9:6) – Christ's divine titles.
- The Suffering Servant (53:5) – Christ's death for our sins.
- The Anointed One (61:1–2) – Fulfilled in Christ's ministry (Luke 4:17–21).
- The Coming King (11:1–10) – Christ's reign of peace and justice.

## Memory Verse

Isaiah 53:5 – "But he was pierced for our transgressions, he was crushed for our iniquities; the punishment that brought us peace was on him, and by his wounds we are healed."

## Reflection Questions

1. What does Isaiah's vision of God's holiness teach us about our need for cleansing?
2. How do the prophecies of judgment and hope balance each other in Isaiah?
3. Why is the prophecy of Immanuel so important for understanding Christ?
4. How does Isaiah 53 deepen your understanding of the cross?

5. How does Isaiah's message of salvation for the nations point us to the mission of the church today?

## Final Exhortation

Students, Isaiah is a book of contrasts: judgment and salvation, despair and hope, sin and holiness. Above all, it is a book that points us to Christ—the Holy One, the Suffering Servant, the Righteous King, and the Redeemer of all nations.

When life feels uncertain, remember the words of Isaiah: "The virgin will conceive... and will call him Immanuel." God is with us. And when sin weighs heavy, remember: "By his wounds we are healed."

May the message of Isaiah draw you closer to the Holy God who judges sin, but who in His mercy has provided salvation through His Son.

# { 24 }

# Jeremiah

The book of Jeremiah is one of the most personal and heart-wrenching in the Old Testament. Known as the "weeping prophet," Jeremiah ministered during Judah's final days before the Babylonian exile. His words are filled with warnings of judgment, laments over sin, and tender promises of restoration.

Jeremiah was called to a difficult task: to speak God's truth to a people who refused to listen. He endured rejection, persecution, imprisonment, and loneliness. Yet through it all, he faithfully proclaimed God's Word. His message shows us that God's holiness demands judgment, but His mercy promises hope—a new covenant written on the heart.

## Background of Jeremiah

- Author: Jeremiah, with his scribe Baruch.
- Date: ~627–586 BC (from Josiah's reign until Jerusalem's fall).
- Setting: Judah under the threat and eventual conquest of Babylon.
- Theme: God's judgment on unrepentant sin, yet hope through His promised new covenant.
- Key Verse: "The heart is deceitful above all things and beyond cure. Who can understand it?" (Jeremiah 17:9)

## Structure of Jeremiah

1. The Call of Jeremiah (Ch. 1)
   ◦ Jeremiah set apart before birth.
2. Oracles of Judgment (Ch. 2–29)
   ◦ Warnings of Judah's idolatry and corruption.
   ◦ Symbolic acts of judgment.
3. The Book of Comfort (Ch. 30–33)
   ◦ Promises of restoration.
   ◦ The new covenant.
4. Judgment on the Nations (Ch. 46–51)
   ◦ God's justice extends to all peoples.
5. The Fall of Jerusalem (Ch. 39, 52)
   ◦ Babylon conquers Judah.
   ◦ Fulfillment of God's Word.

## Key Themes of Jeremiah

1. The Corruption of the Human Heart – Sin is deep and pervasive.
2. God's Relentless Warnings – Judgment comes after patient calls to repent.
3. The Cost of Faithful Ministry – Jeremiah's suffering mirrors God's grief.
4. The New Covenant – God promises transformation of the heart.
5. Hope After Judgment – God's plans are for restoration, not destruction.

## Exposition and Lessons

### 1. The Call of Jeremiah (Ch. 1)

God tells Jeremiah: "Before I formed you in the womb I knew you, before you were born I set you apart" (1:5). Though young and fearful, Jeremiah is empowered by God's Word to uproot, tear down, build, and plant.

Lesson: God calls and equips His servants before they are even born.

### 2. Warnings of Judgment (Ch. 2–29)

Jeremiah denounces Judah's idolatry: "My people have committed two sins: they have forsaken me, the spring of living water, and have dug their own cisterns, broken cisterns that cannot hold water" (2:13). He acts out parables—smashing a clay jar, wearing a yoke, buying a field—to dramatize God's coming judgment.

Lesson: Sin is not just disobedience; it is forsaking the fountain of life for empty substitutes.

### 3. Jeremiah's Lament (Ch. 9, 20)

Jeremiah pours out his grief: "Oh, that my head were a spring of water and my eyes a fountain of tears! I would weep day and night for the slain of my people" (9:1). He struggles with despair, yet clings to God's call.

Lesson: Ministry involves both truth and tears. God's servants share His heart for the lost.

### 4. The Book of Comfort (Ch. 30–33)

Amid warnings, Jeremiah delivers hope: "For I know the plans I have for you... plans to give you hope and a future" (29:11). The climax comes in 31:31–34: God promises a new covenant—not written on stone but on hearts, bringing forgiveness and intimate knowledge of God.

Lesson: Our deepest need is not external reform but inner transformation.

## 5. The Fall of Jerusalem (Ch. 39, 52)

Despite Jeremiah's warnings, Judah resists Babylon, and in 586 BC Jerusalem falls. The temple is burned, the walls destroyed, and the people exiled. Yet even then, Jeremiah holds out hope: God will restore His people after seventy years.

Lesson: God's Word is sure—judgment for sin and hope for the repentant.

## Key Lessons from Jeremiah

1. God calls His servants even before birth.
2. The human heart is deeply sinful and cannot cure itself.
3. Faithful ministry often brings rejection and suffering.
4. God's new covenant promises forgiveness and transformation.
5. Even in judgment, God's plans are for hope and restoration.

## Christ in Jeremiah

- The Fountain of Living Water (2:13) fulfilled in Christ (John 4:14).
- The Good Shepherd (23:4–6) points to Christ, the Righteous Branch.
- The New Covenant (31:31–34) fulfilled in Christ's blood (Luke 22:20).
- Jeremiah's Suffering foreshadows Christ's rejection and grief over Jerusalem.

• Hope of Restoration realized in Christ's kingdom.

## Memory Verse

Jeremiah 31:33 – "This is the covenant I will make with the people of Israel after that time... I will put my law in their minds and write it on their hearts. I will be their God, and they will be my people."

## Reflection Questions

1. What does Jeremiah's call teach us about God's purposes for our lives?
2. How does Jeremiah's grief over sin model faithful ministry today?
3. What does the image of "broken cisterns" teach us about sin?
4. How is the new covenant different from the old covenant?
5. How does Jeremiah point us to Christ as the fulfillment of God's promises?

## Final Exhortation

Students, Jeremiah's life was marked by tears, but also by hope. He reminds us that sin grieves the heart of God, that His Word is sure, and that His love never fails. The promise of the new covenant shows us that true transformation comes not from our efforts but from God writing His law on our hearts through Christ.

When you feel rejected or weary in service, remember Jeremiah. And when you feel broken by sin, remember Christ, who fulfills the new covenant with His blood.

God's plans are still for hope and a future—for Judah in Jeremiah's day, and for us today in Christ.

# { 25 }

# Lamentations

The book of Lamentations is a collection of five poetic laments over the destruction of Jerusalem in 586 BC. Traditionally attributed to Jeremiah, the "weeping prophet," it captures the anguish of God's people as they witness their city burned, their temple destroyed, and their people taken into exile.

This is not a comfortable book. It forces us to face the reality of sin's consequences and the pain of judgment. Yet in the middle of sorrow, a profound hope shines through: "Because of the LORD's great love we are not consumed, for his compassions never fail. They are new every morning; great is your faithfulness" (Lam. 3:22–23).

Lamentations teaches us how to grieve honestly, repent deeply, and hope steadfastly in God's mercy.

## Background of Lamentations

- Author: Traditionally Jeremiah.
- Date: After the fall of Jerusalem, ~586 BC.
- Setting: Jerusalem in ruins.
- Theme: The grief of God's people over sin and judgment, and the hope of God's mercy.
- Key Verse: "Because of the LORD's great love we are not consumed, for his compassions never fail." (Lamentations 3:22)

## Structure of Lamentations

The book is composed of five poems:

1. Chapter 1 – Jerusalem's Desolation: The city personified as a widow.
2. Chapter 2 – God's Anger: The cause of judgment.
3. Chapter 3 – Hope in the Midst of Sorrow: God's faithfulness.
4. Chapter 4 – The Severity of Suffering: The horrors of siege and exile.
5. Chapter 5 – Prayer for Restoration: A corporate cry for mercy.

Each poem (except ch. 5) is an acrostic, structured around the Hebrew alphabet, symbolizing grief expressed completely—from A to Z.

## Key Themes of Lamentations

1. The Consequences of Sin – Jerusalem fell because of unrepentant rebellion.
2. The Reality of Suffering – God's people face deep pain and loss.
3. The Mercy of God – Even in judgment, God's faithfulness shines.
4. The Practice of Lament – Honest prayer includes grief and questions.
5. Hope of Restoration – Sorrow is not the final word.

## Exposition and Lessons

### *1. Jerusalem's Desolation (Ch. 1)*

Jerusalem is described as a widow—once full of people, now desolate. Her allies have betrayed her, and her enemies mock. She acknowledges her sins and the justice of God's judgment.

Lesson: Sin leads to devastation, but acknowledging guilt is the first step toward restoration.

## 2. God's Anger (Ch. 2)

The poet describes God's anger vividly: He has destroyed His own temple, withdrawn His protection, and handed His people over to enemies. This painful truth is clear—God Himself allowed Jerusalem's fall.

Lesson: God's judgment is real and must be taken seriously.

## 3. Hope in the Midst of Sorrow (Ch. 3)

In the middle of grief comes the greatest declaration of hope:

"The steadfast love of the LORD never ceases; his mercies never come to an end; they are new every morning; great is your faithfulness" (3:22–23).

Though the poet feels abandoned, he clings to God's compassion and faithfulness.

Lesson: In suffering, hope is found not in circumstances but in God's unchanging character.

## 4. The Severity of Suffering (Ch. 4)

The horrors of siege are described—children starving, nobles reduced to poverty, priests defiled. Sin has leveled all classes. Yet even in this suffering, God's justice is affirmed.

Lesson: Sin's effects are devastating and indiscriminate; no one escapes its reach.

## 5. Prayer for Restoration (Ch. 5)

The book closes with a communal prayer: "Restore us to yourself, LORD, that we may return; renew our days as of old" (5:21). The final word is not despair but a plea for God's mercy and restoration.

Lesson: Even in judgment, God invites His people to pray and hope for renewal.

## Key Lessons from Lamentations

1. Sin has devastating consequences for individuals and nations.
2. Lament is a biblical way to process grief and suffering.
3. God's mercies are new every morning, even in the darkest times.
4. Hope is grounded in God's faithfulness, not our circumstances.
5. Prayer is the pathway from despair to restoration.

## Christ in Lamentations

- Jerusalem's Suffering foreshadows Christ's weeping over the city (Luke 19:41).
- The Man of Sorrows (Ch. 3) anticipates Christ, who bore grief and suffering.
- God's Mercies fulfilled in Christ, who brings new life each morning.
- The Prayer for Restoration points to Christ, who restores us to God through His cross.

## Memory Verse

Lamentations 3:22–23 – "Because of the LORD's great love we are not consumed, for his compassions never fail. They are new every morning; great is your faithfulness."

## Reflection Questions

1. What does Lamentations teach us about the consequences of sin?
2. How does the practice of lament help us process grief before God?
3. Why is Lamentations 3:22–23 such a powerful statement of hope?
4. How does this book encourage us to pray during seasons of loss?
5. How does Lamentations point us to Christ, the Man of Sorrows?

## Final Exhortation

Students, Lamentations reminds us that sin leads to sorrow, but sorrow can lead us back to God. The poet weeps for Jerusalem, yet in his tears he discovers hope: God's mercies are new every morning.

When you face seasons of loss, grief, or regret, follow the example of Lamentations—weep honestly, confess fully, and cling to God's faithfulness. For Christ, the Man of Sorrows, has borne our griefs and carried our sorrows. In Him, even the darkest night gives way to the dawn of mercy.

{ 26 }

# Ezekiel

The book of Ezekiel is one of the most dramatic and visionary books in the Bible. Written by a priest turned prophet during the Babylonian exile, it combines powerful symbolic actions, vivid visions, and profound promises of restoration.

Ezekiel's message is clear: God is holy, His glory is supreme, and His people must repent. While the first half of the book emphasizes judgment for sin, the second half overflows with hope—God promises to restore His people, give them a new heart and Spirit, and one day bring them into a renewed land under a perfect Shepherd.

Though written in exile, Ezekiel reminds us that God's throne is not bound to one place. His glory fills the heavens, and His purposes extend beyond national defeat to eternal victory.

## Background of Ezekiel

- Author: Ezekiel, a priest and prophet.
- Date: ~593–571 BC.
- Setting: Babylon during the exile.
- Theme: God's glory revealed in judgment and restoration.
- Key Verse: "I will give you a new heart and put a new spirit in you." (Ezekiel 36:26)

## Structure of Ezekiel

1. The Call and Visions of God's Glory (Ch. 1–3)
    ◦ The vision of God's throne.
    ◦ Ezekiel's commission as prophet.
2. Judgment on Judah and Jerusalem (Ch. 4–24)
    ◦ Symbolic acts of judgment.
    ◦ God's glory departs from the temple.
3. Judgment on the Nations (Ch. 25–32)
    ◦ Oracles against Ammon, Moab, Edom, Egypt, Tyre, and others.
4. Promise of Restoration (Ch. 33–39)
    ◦ God's shepherd for His people.
    ◦ Vision of dry bones.
    ◦ Promise of a new heart and Spirit.
5. The Vision of the New Temple (Ch. 40–48)
    ◦ Detailed vision of a future temple.
    ◦ God's glory returns.
    ◦ Promise of God dwelling with His people.

## Key Themes of Ezekiel

1. The Glory of God – God's presence is supreme and holy.
2. Individual Responsibility – Each person is accountable before God.
3. Judgment and Exile – Sin leads to discipline and loss.
4. Restoration and Renewal – God promises a new heart, Spirit, and Shepherd.
5. God Dwelling with His People – The final vision points to God's eternal presence.

## Exposition and Lessons

### 1. The Vision of God's Glory (Ch. 1–3)

Ezekiel sees a vision of God's throne—wheels within wheels, living creatures, and a radiant figure like fire and light. Overwhelmed, he falls facedown. This vision of glory shapes his entire ministry.

Lesson: Ministry begins with a vision of God's majesty. Without it, we cannot endure trials.

### 2. Symbolic Acts and Judgment (Ch. 4–24)

Ezekiel acts out God's judgment—lying on his side for days, shaving his head, cooking food over dung. These symbolic acts demonstrate the seriousness of sin. Most tragically, Ezekiel sees the glory of God departing from the temple (Ch. 10).

Lesson: Sin drives away God's presence, but judgment is never the end of the story.

### 3. Judgment on the Nations (Ch. 25–32)

God declares judgment not only on Judah but on surrounding nations. Their pride, violence, and idolatry bring destruction. God's sovereignty extends over all kingdoms.

Lesson: God is not just Israel's God—He rules the nations.

### 4. Promise of Restoration (Ch. 33–39)

Ezekiel becomes a watchman, warning the people. He delivers promises of hope:

- The Good Shepherd (Ch. 34) – God Himself will shepherd His people and place over them "one Shepherd, my servant David."

- The Valley of Dry Bones (Ch. 37) – Ezekiel sees a valley of skeletons come to life, symbolizing Israel's restoration.
- A New Heart and Spirit (Ch. 36) – God promises inner transformation: "I will remove your heart of stone and give you a heart of flesh."

Lesson: God not only restores circumstances but transforms hearts.

### 5. The Vision of the New Temple (Ch. 40–48)

Ezekiel closes with an elaborate vision of a new temple and a restored land. The most glorious moment comes when God's presence returns: "The glory of the LORD filled the temple" (43:5). The book ends with the promise: "The LORD is there" (48:35).

Lesson: The ultimate hope is God's presence dwelling with His people forever.

### Key Lessons from Ezekiel

1. God's glory is supreme and demands reverence.
2. Sin removes us from God's presence, but repentance leads to renewal.
3. Every individual is accountable before God.
4. God promises not only restoration but transformation through a new heart and Spirit.
5. The final hope is God dwelling with His people eternally.

### Christ in Ezekiel

- The Good Shepherd (34:23) – Fulfilled in Christ, the Good Shepherd (John 10:11).

- The New Heart and Spirit (36:26) – Fulfilled through the Holy Spirit in the New Covenant.
- The Valley of Dry Bones (37) – Fulfilled in Christ's resurrection power, giving new life.
- The Glory Returning to the Temple (43) – Fulfilled in Christ, God's glory in flesh (John 1:14).
- "The LORD is There" (48:35) – Fulfilled in Christ, Immanuel, "God with us."

## Memory Verse

Ezekiel 36:26 – "I will give you a new heart and put a new spirit in you; I will remove from you your heart of stone and give you a heart of flesh."

## Reflection Questions

1. What does Ezekiel's vision of God's glory teach us about His holiness?
2. How do Ezekiel's symbolic acts help us grasp the seriousness of sin?
3. What hope does the promise of a new heart and Spirit give us today?
4. How does the vision of dry bones illustrate God's power to restore life?
5. How does Ezekiel point us to Christ as Shepherd, Savior, and God's glory revealed?

## Final Exhortation

Students, Ezekiel is a book of both sobering judgment and breathtaking hope. It reminds us that God's glory is too holy to ignore, and that sin brings separation. But it also promises a new heart, a new Spirit, and a new Shepherd who will never abandon His flock.

For us, that promise is fulfilled in Christ. He is the Good Shepherd, the giver of new life, the One who fills us with His Spirit, and the assurance that God is with us.

So remember the final words of Ezekiel: "The LORD is there." May that truth anchor your faith through judgment, exile, and restoration—because in Christ, God's presence will never leave you.

## { 27 }

# Daniel

The book of Daniel is one of the most inspiring and prophetic books in all of Scripture. It combines historical narrative with apocalyptic visions, reminding us that God is sovereign over kings and kingdoms and that He will ultimately establish His eternal reign.

Daniel was taken as a young man into exile in Babylon, yet he remained faithful to God in a pagan culture. His life models uncompromising integrity, courageous prayer, and unshakable trust in God. The second half of the book gives us breathtaking visions of world empires, the coming of the Son of Man, and God's final victory.

Daniel teaches us how to live faithfully in exile while keeping our eyes fixed on God's eternal kingdom.

### Background of Daniel

- Author: Daniel, a Hebrew exile in Babylon.
- Date: Events span ~605–536 BC (Babylonian exile and early Persian period).
- Setting: Captivity in Babylon and later under Persian rule.
- Theme: God rules over history and His kingdom will prevail.
- Key Verse: "The God of heaven will set up a kingdom that will never be destroyed." (Daniel 2:44)

## Structure of Daniel

1. Daniel and His Friends in Exile (Ch. 1–6)
    ◦ Faithfulness in Babylon.
    ◦ God's deliverance from danger.
2. Daniel's Visions of the Future (Ch. 7–12)
    ◦ Four beasts and the Ancient of Days.
    ◦ Prophecies of kingdoms.
    ◦ The Son of Man and the end times.

## Key Themes of Daniel

1. God's Sovereignty – He rules over kings and kingdoms.
2. Faithfulness in Exile – God's people can live holy lives in a hostile culture.
3. God's Deliverance – He rescues those who trust Him.
4. Prophecy of the Messiah – The Son of Man and the Anointed One.
5. The Coming Kingdom – God's eternal reign is certain.

## Exposition and Lessons

### 1. Faithfulness in Babylon (Ch. 1)

Daniel and his friends refuse to defile themselves with the king's food. God blesses their obedience, giving them wisdom and favor.

Lesson: Holiness in small choices prepares us for greater tests of faith.

### 2. God Reveals Mysteries (Ch. 2)

Nebuchadnezzar's dream of a statue representing world empires is interpreted by Daniel. God reveals that human kingdoms rise and fall, but His kingdom will endure forever.

Lesson: History is not random—God directs it toward His eternal purpose.

### 3. The Fiery Furnace (Ch. 3)l

Shadrach, Meshach, and Abednego refuse to worship the golden image. They are thrown into a fiery furnace but delivered by a fourth figure—one like the Son of God.

Lesson: God's presence sustains us in trials, and His power delivers us from the flames.

### 4. The Writing on the Wall (Ch. 5)

Belshazzar mocks God by drinking from the temple vessels. A mysterious hand writes judgment on the wall: "MENE, MENE, TEKEL, PARSIN." That very night Babylon falls.

Lesson: Pride brings downfall; God humbles kings who defy Him.

### 5. The Lions' Den (Ch. 6)

Daniel continues to pray despite the king's decree. He is thrown into the lions' den but delivered by God's angel.

Lesson: Prayer is worth the cost, for God is faithful to His servants.

### 6. The Ancient of Days and the Son of Man (Ch. 7)

Daniel's vision of four beasts represents world empires. But the scene shifts to heaven: the Ancient of Days sits on His throne, and the Son of Man is given everlasting dominion.

Lesson: Earthly kingdoms are temporary; Christ's kingdom is eternal.

## 7. The Prophecy of the Anointed One (Ch. 9)

Daniel prays for his people, and God reveals the prophecy of seventy "weeks." This points to the coming of the Anointed One, who will bring atonement and establish righteousness.

Lesson: God has a plan for redemption that centers on Christ.

## 8. The Time of the End (Ch. 10–12)

Daniel receives visions of coming conflicts, persecution, and ultimate deliverance. The faithful will rise to everlasting life, while others to shame and contempt.

Lesson: History ends not with chaos but with resurrection and God's final victory.

### Key Lessons from Daniel

1. God is sovereign over history, rulers, and nations.
2. Faithfulness in exile requires courage, prayer, and conviction.
3. God delivers His people in trials according to His will.
4. Christ, the Son of Man, will reign forever.
5. Our ultimate hope is resurrection and eternal life with God.

### Christ in Daniel

- The Son of Man (7:13–14) – Fulfilled in Christ, who receives eternal dominion.
- The Fourth Man in the Fire (3:25) – A picture of Christ's presence with His people.
- The Anointed One (9:25–26) – Prophecy of Christ's coming and atoning work.
- The Resurrection (12:2) – Fulfilled in Christ, the firstborn from the dead.

- The Everlasting Kingdom (2:44) – Fulfilled in Christ's eternal reign.

## Memory Verse

Daniel 2:44 – "The God of heaven will set up a kingdom that will never be destroyed, nor will it be left to another people. It will crush all those kingdoms and bring them to an end, but it will itself endure forever."

## Reflection Questions

1. How does Daniel's example teach us to live faithfully in a secular culture?
2. What does Nebuchadnezzar's dream teach us about the rise and fall of kingdoms?
3. How does the fiery furnace show us God's presence in trials?
4. Why is the vision of the Son of Man central to understanding Christ?
5. How does Daniel's prophecy of resurrection shape our hope today?

## Final Exhortation

Students, the book of Daniel teaches us to stand firm in faith, even when surrounded by opposition. Like Daniel and his friends, we are called to live with integrity, pray with boldness, and trust God's sovereignty.

Though kingdoms rise and fall, God's kingdom will endure forever. Though trials come, Christ is with us in the fire. And though death threatens, resurrection awaits.

So lift your eyes above the shifting kingdoms of this world and fix them on the Son of Man, whose dominion is everlasting and whose kingdom will never be destroyed.

# { 28 }

# Hosea

The book of Hosea is one of the most striking and emotional in all the prophets. God commands Hosea to live out a message that reflects His relationship with Israel. Hosea marries Gomer, a woman unfaithful to him, symbolizing Israel's unfaithfulness to God. Yet Hosea pursues her in love, reflecting God's relentless grace toward His people.

Hosea's life shows us that God's covenant love is not a contract to be broken but a commitment that endures even in betrayal. Israel's idolatry and spiritual adultery brought judgment, but God's love would not let them go. His desire was not punishment for punishment's sake but restoration.

This book reminds us of the depth of our sin and the even greater depth of God's redeeming love.

### Background of Hosea

- Author: Hosea, a prophet in the Northern Kingdom.
- Date: ~755–715 BC.
- Setting: Israel during a time of prosperity but deep idolatry, shortly before the Assyrian conquest (722 BC).
- Theme: God's faithful love in contrast to Israel's unfaithfulness.
- Key Verse: "I will heal their waywardness and love them freely, for my anger has turned away from them." (Hosea 14:4)

## Structure of Hosea

1. Hosea's Marriage and Children (Ch. 1–3)
    ◦ Hosea marries Gomer, an unfaithful wife.
    ◦ Children's names symbolize judgment and hope.
    ◦ Hosea redeems Gomer.
2. God's Case Against Israel (Ch. 4–13)
    ◦ Accusations of idolatry and injustice.
    ◦ Warnings of judgment.
3. Promise of Restoration (Ch. 14)
    ◦ God promises healing and renewal for the repentant.

## Key Themes of Hosea

1. God's Covenant Love – A faithful love that endures betrayal.
2. Spiritual Adultery – Idolatry is unfaithfulness to God.
3. Judgment and Consequences – Sin brings devastation.
4. Redemption and Restoration – God's love pursues and heals.
5. Love Beyond Law – God's mercy is greater than human sin.

## Exposition and Lessons

### 1. Hosea's Marriage (Ch. 1–3)

God commands Hosea to marry Gomer, a woman who would be unfaithful. Their marriage becomes a living parable of God and Israel. Hosea's children are named "Jezreel" (judgment), "Lo-Ruhamah" (not loved), and "Lo-Ammi" (not my people). Yet in mercy, God promises reversal: "You are my people"; and they will say, "You are my God" (2:23).

Lesson: God's covenant love remains steadfast even when His people are unfaithful.

## 2. God's Case Against Israel (Ch. 4–13)

God accuses Israel of idolatry, immorality, and injustice: "There is no faithfulness, no love, no acknowledgment of God in the land" (4:1). They turn to Baal and foreign alliances for security. Like an unfaithful spouse, they betray their covenant with God.

Lesson: Idolatry is not just bowing to idols but trusting in anything other than God.

## 3. Hosea's Plea for Repentance (Ch. 6)

Hosea calls the people: "Come, let us return to the LORD" (6:1). God desires mercy, not sacrifice; knowledge of God rather than empty rituals (6:6).

Lesson: God values authentic relationship over empty religion.

## 4. The Judgment of God (Ch. 8–10)

Hosea warns that Israel will reap what they sow: "They sow the wind and reap the whirlwind" (8:7). Their false worship will bring destruction. Ultimately, Assyria will conquer them.

Lesson: Sin carries consequences; turning from God leads to ruin.

## 5. The Promise of Restoration (Ch. 14)

The book ends not with despair but with hope: "Return, Israel, to the LORD your God" (14:1). God promises to heal their waywardness, love them freely, and cause them to flourish like a fruitful vineyard.

Lesson: God's final word is not judgment but redemption.

### Key Lessons from Hosea

1. God's love is faithful even when we are not.
2. Idolatry is spiritual adultery—giving our hearts to false gods.

3. Empty religion without love for God is worthless.
4. Sin brings real consequences, but repentance brings healing.
5. God's covenant love relentlessly pursues restoration.

## Christ in Hosea

- The Faithful Husband (Ch. 3) – Christ is the Bridegroom who redeems His unfaithful bride, the church.
- The Reversal of Judgment (1:10–11) – Fulfilled in Christ, who makes us God's people.
- "I desire mercy, not sacrifice" (6:6) – Quoted by Jesus in Matthew 9:13.
- The Redeemer's Love – Christ gave Himself to purchase His bride from slavery to sin.
- Restoration and Healing (14:4) – Fulfilled in Christ, who heals our backsliding.

## Memory Verse

Hosea 14:4 – "I will heal their waywardness and love them freely, for my anger has turned away from them."

## Reflection Questions

1. How does Hosea's marriage illustrate God's relationship with His people?
2. What are modern forms of "spiritual adultery" we must guard against?
3. Why does God desire mercy and knowledge of Him rather than sacrifice?
4. What does Hosea teach us about the consequences of sin?
5. How does Hosea point us to Christ, the faithful Bridegroom?

## Final Exhortation

Students, Hosea reveals the heart of God like few other books. His love is not cold law but burning covenant affection. He does not abandon His people even when they are unfaithful. Instead, He pursues them, redeems them, and restores them.

In Christ, this love is made complete. He is the Bridegroom who gave His life to win back His unfaithful bride. His love is relentless, redeeming, and everlasting.

So let Hosea remind you: God's love is greater than your sin, and His desire is not to cast you away but to heal you and call you His own once again.

# { 29 }

# Joel

The book of Joel is a short but powerful prophecy that speaks about crisis, repentance, and renewal. Joel ministered during a devastating locust plague that had stripped Israel's land bare. He used this natural disaster as a picture of an even greater reality: the coming Day of the LORD.

Joel's message is both sobering and hopeful. God calls His people to heartfelt repentance, not empty rituals. At the same time, He promises an outpouring of His Spirit, blessings of restoration, and ultimate deliverance for those who call upon His name. Joel bridges judgment with the hope of revival, pointing us forward to Pentecost and the coming kingdom of Christ.

## Background of Joel

- Author: Joel, son of Pethuel.
- Date: Difficult to date; possibly 9th–5th century BC.
- Setting: Judah after a devastating locust plague.
- Theme: The Day of the Lord brings judgment for sin but also blessing and restoration for the repentant.
- Key Verse: "Everyone who calls on the name of the LORD will be saved." (Joel 2:32)

## Structure of Joel

1. The Locust Plague and Call to Repentance (Ch. 1)
   - A national disaster.
   - A summons to prayer and fasting.
2. The Day of the Lord (Ch. 2:1–17)
   - The plague as a foreshadowing of God's coming judgment.
   - Call for true repentance.
3. God's Response: Restoration and Spirit Outpouring (Ch. 2:18–32)
   - God promises renewal of land and people.
   - Promise of the Holy Spirit.
4. Final Judgment and Deliverance (Ch. 3)
   - Judgment on the nations.
   - Blessing for God's people in Zion.

## Key Themes of Joel

1. The Day of the Lord – A day of judgment and salvation.
2. The Call to Repentance – Return to God with all your heart.
3. The Outpouring of the Spirit – God promises His Spirit for all believers.
4. Judgment of Nations – God will hold all peoples accountable.
5. Restoration of God's People – God turns devastation into blessing.

## Exposition and Lessons

### 1. The Locust Plague (Ch. 1)

Joel describes a plague of locusts that devastated the land: "What the locust swarm has left the great locusts have eaten" (1:4). He calls priests, elders, and all people to weep and fast, recognizing God's judgment.

Lesson: Disasters can serve as wake-up calls, reminding us to seek God's face.

### 2. The Day of the Lord (Ch. 2:1–17)

Joel uses the locust plague as a foreshadowing of a greater judgment—the Day of the Lord. He warns: "The day of the LORD is great; it is dreadful. Who can endure it?" (2:11). Yet he offers hope: "Return to me with all your heart, with fasting and weeping and mourning" (2:12).

Lesson: God desires repentance from the heart, not outward show.

### 3. The Promise of Restoration (Ch. 2:18–27)

When the people repent, God promises to restore their land: "I will repay you for the years the locusts have eaten" (2:25). The devastation will be reversed with abundance, joy, and peace.

Lesson: God not only forgives but restores what sin and suffering have stolen.

### 4. The Outpouring of the Spirit (Ch. 2:28–32)

Joel delivers a groundbreaking promise: "I will pour out my Spirit on all people. Your sons and daughters will prophesy, your old men will dream dreams, your young men will see visions" (2:28). This was fulfilled at Pentecost (Acts 2), when the Holy Spirit empowered the church.

Lesson: God's Spirit is available to all who call on His name.

## 5. Final Judgment and Blessing (Ch. 3)

Joel concludes with a vision of God gathering the nations for judgment in the Valley of Jehoshaphat. But for His people, blessing and security will flow: "The LORD will be a refuge for his people" (3:16).

Lesson: God's judgment is real, but His people will find refuge in Him.

### Key Lessons from Joel

1. The Day of the Lord is both a warning and a promise.
2. True repentance is heartfelt, not superficial.
3. God restores what is lost when we return to Him.
4. The Holy Spirit empowers all believers for service.
5. God will judge the nations, but His people will find refuge in Him.

### Christ in Joel

- The Day of the Lord fulfilled in Christ's coming—both in judgment and salvation.
- The Outpouring of the Spirit (2:28) fulfilled at Pentecost through Christ's resurrection and ascension.
- The Call to Salvation (2:32) fulfilled in Christ: "Everyone who calls on the name of the Lord will be saved."
- God's Refuge (3:16) fulfilled in Christ, our shelter and Savior.
- The Restorer (2:25) fulfilled in Christ, who restores the years sin has stolen.

### Memory Verse

Joel 2:32 – "Everyone who calls on the name of the LORD will be saved."

## Reflection Questions

1. How does Joel connect natural disasters to spiritual lessons?
2. What does it mean to "return to God with all your heart"?
3. How has God restored areas of your life that were broken?
4. Why is Joel 2:28–32 so important for understanding the work of the Holy Spirit?
5. How does the message of Joel encourage the church today?

## Final Exhortation

Students, Joel teaches us that the Day of the Lord is both a day of judgment and a day of salvation. It warns us of the seriousness of sin but also invites us into God's mercy and blessing.

The locusts remind us of sin's devastation, but God's promise of restoration reminds us that He can bring life from loss. And the outpouring of the Spirit shows us that in Christ, God has given us power to live, witness, and hope until He comes again.

So let us heed Joel's call: return to the Lord with all our hearts, live in the fullness of His Spirit, and look forward to the day when His kingdom comes in glory.

# 30

# Obadiah

The book of Obadiah may be the shortest book in the Old Testament, but its message is weighty and enduring. In just 21 verses, God pronounces judgment on the nation of Edom for its pride and cruelty toward Judah, while also declaring the certainty of His coming kingdom.

Obadiah teaches us that God notices how nations and individuals treat one another. Pride and violence bring downfall, but God's justice ensures that His people will be vindicated. The book ends with a powerful hope: "And the kingdom will be the LORD's" (Obadiah 21).

Though short, Obadiah speaks volumes about the dangers of pride, the certainty of judgment, and the triumph of God's kingdom.

## Background of Obadiah

- Author: Obadiah (meaning "servant of the LORD").
- Date: Likely ~586 BC, after the fall of Jerusalem.
- Setting: Judah devastated by Babylon, with Edom taking advantage of their suffering.
- Theme: God judges Edom's pride and violence, but promises deliverance and victory for His people.
- Key Verse: "The pride of your heart has deceived you." (Obadiah 3)

## Structure of Obadiah

1. Judgment on Edom (v. 1–14)
   ◦ Pride and arrogance exposed.
   ◦ Violence against Judah condemned.
2. The Day of the Lord (v. 15–18)
   ◦ Judgment extends to all nations.
   ◦ Retribution according to deeds.
3. The Deliverance of Zion (v. 19–21)
   ◦ Israel's restoration.
   ◦ The Lord's kingdom established.

## Key Themes of Obadiah

1. The Danger of Pride – Self-reliance leads to downfall.
2. God's Justice – Nations are accountable to God for their actions.
3. Brotherhood Betrayed – Edom failed in its duty toward Judah, its "brother nation."
4. The Day of the Lord – God's judgment will come upon all who oppose Him.
5. The Triumph of God's Kingdom – In the end, the kingdom belongs to the Lord.

## Exposition and Lessons

### 1. The Pride of Edom (v. 1–4)

Edom, descendants of Esau, lived in the rocky strongholds of Mount Seir. They trusted their natural defenses and allies, boasting in their security. But God declared: "Though you soar like the eagle and make your nest among the stars, from there I will bring you down" (v. 4).

Lesson: Pride blinds us to our dependence on God and always precedes a fall.

## 2. Violence Against Judah (v. 10–14)

When Babylon invaded Jerusalem, Edom not only failed to help their "brother" Judah but also rejoiced over their downfall and looted their city. God condemned their betrayal.

Lesson: God holds us accountable for how we treat others, especially in times of their vulnerability.

## 3. The Day of the Lord (v. 15–18)

Obadiah declares: "The day of the LORD is near for all nations. As you have done, it will be done to you" (v. 15). Edom's judgment was a preview of God's justice for all nations.

Lesson: The Day of the Lord is certain—judgment and justice will come to all.

## 4. Deliverance and Restoration (v. 19–21)

The prophecy ends with hope. God's people will possess their land again, and "deliverers will go up on Mount Zion to govern the mountains of Esau. And the kingdom will be the LORD's" (v. 21).

Lesson: History does not end with human pride or conflict—it ends with God's kingdom triumphing.

### Key Lessons from Obadiah

1. Pride deceives and leads to downfall.
2. God notices injustice and holds nations accountable.
3. Betrayal of "brothers" brings God's judgment.
4. The Day of the Lord brings both judgment and vindication.

5. God's kingdom is the final and eternal reality.

## Christ in Obadiah

- The Betrayed Brother – Israel betrayed by Edom points to Christ betrayed by His own people.
- The Judge of Nations – Fulfilled in Christ, who will judge all nations in righteousness.
- The Deliverer from Zion (v. 21) – Fulfilled in Christ, who brings salvation from Mount Zion.
- The Kingdom is the Lord's – Fulfilled in Christ's eternal reign (Revelation 11:15).
- The Hope of Restoration – Fulfilled in Christ, who restores His people to their inheritance.

## Memory Verse

Obadiah 21 – "The deliverers will go up on Mount Zion to govern the mountains of Esau. And the kingdom will be the LORD's."

## Reflection Questions

1. How does pride deceive us, as it did Edom?
2. Why was Edom's betrayal of Judah so serious in God's eyes?
3. How does Obadiah expand the vision of judgment to include all nations?
4. What hope does Obadiah give about the future of God's people?
5. How does this short book point us to Christ and His kingdom?

## Final Exhortation

Students, Obadiah reminds us that no one is beyond God's justice. Pride, betrayal, and injustice will not go unpunished. But for God's people, there is hope beyond judgment—the triumph of His eternal kingdom.

Edom's fall is a warning, but also a reassurance: God's justice is sure, and His promises are unshakable. The final word is this: "The kingdom will be the LORD's."

In Christ, that kingdom has come and will one day be revealed in its fullness. Let Obadiah encourage you to live humbly, act justly, and place your hope in the everlasting reign of our Lord.

# 31

# Jonah

The book of Jonah is one of the most well-known stories in Scripture, yet it is often misunderstood. Many remember it as the story of a prophet swallowed by a great fish, but at its heart, Jonah is about the boundless mercy of God.

Jonah's mission was to call the people of Nineveh, Israel's enemies, to repentance. But Jonah resisted because he knew God would be merciful. His struggle mirrors ours when we desire judgment for others but mercy for ourselves. Jonah shows us the wideness of God's compassion—He desires all people to repent and be saved.

Ultimately, Jonah points us to Christ, who also spent three days in the depths but rose again to bring salvation to the nations.

### Background of Jonah

- Author: Traditionally Jonah, son of Amittai.
- Date: ~8th century BC, during the reign of Jeroboam II.
- Setting: The Assyrian capital, Nineveh, a powerful and cruel empire.
- Theme: God's mercy extends to all nations, even to those considered enemies.
- Key Verse: "Salvation comes from the LORD." (Jonah 2:9)

## Structure of Jonah

1. Jonah's Call and Flight (Ch. 1)
    - Jonah flees from God's command.
    - A storm and a great fish.
2. Jonah's Prayer of Deliverance (Ch. 2)
    - Jonah prays from the belly of the fish.
    - God delivers him.
3. Jonah's Preaching in Nineveh (Ch. 3)
    - Jonah obeys and preaches repentance.
    - Nineveh repents.
4. Jonah's Anger and God's Mercy (Ch. 4)
    - Jonah resents God's compassion.
    - God teaches him with a plant and a worm.

## Key Themes of Jonah

1. The Mercy of God – His compassion extends to all people.
2. The Struggle of Obedience – Jonah resists God's call but cannot escape.
3. Repentance and Forgiveness – Even wicked Nineveh repents and receives mercy.
4. God's Sovereignty – He controls wind, waves, fish, plants, and nations.
5. The Universality of Salvation – God's grace is not limited to Israel.

## Exposition and Lessons

### 1. Jonah's Call and Rebellion (Ch. 1)

God commands Jonah: "Go to the great city of Nineveh and preach against it" (1:2). Instead, Jonah flees toward Tarshish, trying to escape God's presence. A storm threatens the ship, and Jonah is thrown into the sea, where a great fish swallows him.

Lesson: We cannot run from God's call; disobedience always brings storms.

### 2. Jonah's Prayer (Ch. 2)

From inside the fish, Jonah prays: "In my distress I called to the LORD, and he answered me" (2:2). He acknowledges God's salvation: "Salvation comes from the LORD" (2:9). God delivers him, and the fish spits him onto dry land.

Lesson: Even in our lowest moments, God hears and delivers when we repent.

### 3. Nineveh Repents (Ch. 3)

Jonah preaches a short message: "Forty more days and Nineveh will be overthrown" (3:4). Amazingly, the entire city—from king to commoner—repents with fasting and sackcloth. God spares them.

Lesson: No one is beyond God's mercy; true repentance brings forgiveness.

### 4. Jonah's Anger (Ch. 4)

Instead of rejoicing, Jonah is angry that God spared Nineveh. He says: "Isn't this what I said, LORD? That is why I tried to forestall by fleeing to Tarshish. I knew that you are a gracious and compassionate God" (4:2). God teaches him with a plant that grows to give shade and then withers, showing Jonah his misplaced compassion.

Lesson: God's mercy is not ours to control—it extends even to our enemies.

## Key Lessons from Jonah

1. You cannot outrun God's call or presence.
2. God's mercy reaches even the most wicked when they repent.
3. Salvation is God's work, not ours—"Salvation comes from the Lord."
4. Our hearts must be shaped by God's compassion, not our prejudice.
5. God's mission is global—His love is for all nations.

## Christ in Jonah

- Three Days in the Fish (Ch. 2) – A picture of Christ's death and resurrection (Matthew 12:40).
- The Preacher of Repentance – Fulfilled in Christ, who proclaimed repentance and forgiveness.
- Salvation of the Nations – Jonah foreshadows Christ's mission to bring salvation beyond Israel.
- The Compassion of God – Fully revealed in Christ's mercy toward sinners.
- The Greater Jonah – Christ obeyed perfectly where Jonah failed.

## Memory Verse

Jonah 2:9 – "But I, with shouts of grateful praise, will sacrifice to you. What I have vowed I will make good. I will say, 'Salvation comes from the LORD.'"

## Reflection Questions

1. Why did Jonah resist God's call to go to Nineveh?
2. What does Jonah's prayer teach us about repentance and God's mercy?

3. Why is Nineveh's response to Jonah's preaching so significant?

4. How does Jonah's anger reveal the struggle between human prejudice and God's compassion?

5. How does Jonah point us to Christ, the greater Prophet?

## Final Exhortation

Students, Jonah shows us that God's mercy is greater than our failures and wider than our boundaries. He pursues not only runaway prophets but also rebellious nations. He desires that all people—yes, even our enemies—turn to Him and live.

When you feel like running, remember Jonah: God's call will find you. When you think someone is too far gone, remember Nineveh: God's mercy can reach anyone. And when you wrestle with resentment, remember God's heart: He is gracious, compassionate, slow to anger, and abounding in love.

Christ is the greater Jonah. He went willingly, endured three days in the depths, and rose again to bring salvation to all. Let Jonah's story inspire you to embrace God's mission and reflect His mercy to the world.

{ 32 }

# Micah

The book of Micah delivers a bold and balanced message: judgment for sin and hope through God's mercy. Micah, a contemporary of Isaiah, ministered to both Israel (the northern kingdom) and Judah (the southern kingdom) during a time of corruption, injustice, and idolatry.

Micah speaks out against the powerful who exploited the poor, leaders who perverted justice, and priests who served for money. Yet in the midst of warnings, Micah delivers some of the most beautiful promises of the Messiah, including the prophecy that He would be born in Bethlehem (Micah 5:2).

Micah shows us that God requires more than ritual—He desires justice, mercy, and humility. And He assures us that God's mercy triumphs over judgment, pointing us to Christ, the Shepherd-King.

## Background of Micah

- Author: Micah of Moresheth.
- Date: ~740–700 BC.
- Setting: Israel and Judah during times of political upheaval, social injustice, and false religion.
- Theme: God judges sin but promises deliverance through the Messiah.

- Key Verse: "He has shown you, O mortal, what is good. And what does the LORD require of you? To act justly and to love mercy and to walk humbly with your God." (Micah 6:8)

## Structure of Micah

1. Judgment on Israel and Judah (Ch. 1–3)
    ◦ Accusations of idolatry and injustice.
    ◦ Corruption of leaders and prophets.
2. Promise of Restoration (Ch. 4–5)
    ◦ The mountain of the Lord's house.
    ◦ The Messiah born in Bethlehem.
3. God's Case Against His People (Ch. 6)
    ◦ A covenant lawsuit.
    ◦ Call to justice, mercy, and humility.
4. Hope and Mercy (Ch. 7)
    ◦ Confession of sin.
    ◦ God's mercy and forgiveness.

## Key Themes of Micah

1. God's Judgment – Against idolatry, corruption, and injustice.
2. True Religion – Not rituals but justice, mercy, and humility.
3. The Coming Messiah – Born in Bethlehem, He will shepherd His people.
4. God's Mercy – His compassion is greater than sin.
5. Hope Beyond Judgment – Restoration is certain through God's promises.

## Exposition and Lessons

### 1. Judgment on Sin (Ch. 1–3)

Micah condemns Israel and Judah for idolatry and oppression: "They covet fields and seize them, and houses, and take them" (2:2). Leaders pervert justice, and prophets preach for money. God declares judgment and destruction, including the fall of Samaria and Jerusalem's devastation.

Lesson: God will not overlook injustice or corruption, especially among leaders.

### 2. The Mountain of the Lord (Ch. 4)

Micah envisions a future where the nations stream to the mountain of the Lord, seeking His ways. Swords will be beaten into plowshares, and peace will reign.

Lesson: God's ultimate plan is peace and justice through His kingdom.

### 3. The Coming Messiah (Ch. 5)

Micah prophesies: "But you, Bethlehem Ephrathah, though you are small among the clans of Judah, out of you will come for me one who will be ruler over Israel" (5:2). This Messiah will shepherd His flock in strength and bring peace.

Lesson: God's hope for the world is found in Christ, the Shepherd-King from Bethlehem.

### 4. What God Requires (Ch. 6)

God brings a covenant lawsuit, asking: "My people, what have I done to you? How have I burdened you?" (6:3). The people ask if sacrifices will please God, but Micah answers: "To act justly and to love mercy and to walk humbly with your God" (6:8).

Lesson: God desires a transformed life, not empty rituals.

### 5. Hope in God's Mercy (Ch. 7)

Micah laments the sin of the people but ends with hope: "Who is a God like you, who pardons sin and forgives the transgression... You will again have compassion on us" (7:18–19).

Lesson: God's mercy triumphs over judgment, offering forgiveness and restoration.

## Key Lessons from Micah

1. God will judge injustice, idolatry, and corruption.
2. True religion is not ritual but living justly, mercifully, and humbly.
3. The Messiah, born in Bethlehem, fulfills God's promises.
4. God's mercy is greater than our sin.
5. Hope is certain because God delights in compassion.

## Christ in Micah

- The Ruler from Bethlehem (5:2) – Fulfilled in Christ's birth.
- The Shepherd-King (5:4) – Fulfilled in Christ, who shepherds His flock.
- The Mountain of the Lord (4:1–4) – Fulfilled in Christ's kingdom bringing peace.
- Justice, Mercy, Humility (6:8) – Perfectly embodied in Christ's life and teaching.
- God's Compassion (7:18–19) – Fulfilled in Christ's forgiveness of sins.

## Memory Verse

Micah 6:8 – "He has shown you, O mortal, what is good. And what does the LORD require of you? To act justly and to love mercy and to walk humbly with your God."

## Reflection Questions

1. What injustices in Micah's time led to God's judgment?
2. How does Micah 5:2 point directly to Christ's birth?
3. What does Micah 6:8 teach us about true worship?
4. How do Micah's words of mercy in chapter 7 comfort us today?
5. How does Christ fulfill Micah's vision of justice, mercy, and peace?

## Final Exhortation

Students, Micah reminds us that God sees both the corruption of leaders and the suffering of the oppressed. He calls His people to live not by empty rituals but by justice, mercy, and humility.

At the same time, Micah assures us of hope—the Messiah from Bethlehem who would shepherd His people and bring peace. This prophecy finds its fulfillment in Christ, the King of kings who rules with justice and compassion.

So let Micah's message shape your life: act justly, love mercy, walk humbly, and place your hope in the Shepherd-King whose mercy never fails.

# { 33 }

# Nahum

The book of Nahum is a prophecy of judgment against the city of Nineveh, the capital of Assyria. About 100 years earlier, Jonah had preached in Nineveh and the people repented. But by Nahum's time, the repentance had faded, and Nineveh had returned to its cruelty, violence, and idolatry.

Nahum's message is clear: God is patient, but He will not let sin go unpunished. Assyria, once an instrument of God's judgment against Israel, would itself be judged for its arrogance and brutality. At the same time, Nahum brings comfort to God's people by assuring them of His justice and protection.

This book reminds us that God's justice may seem delayed, but it is certain. Nations and individuals alike will answer to Him.

## Background of Nahum

- Author: Nahum ("comfort" or "consolation").
- Date: ~663–612 BC, likely before Nineveh's fall in 612 BC.
- Setting: Assyria at the height of its power, oppressing surrounding nations.
- Theme: God is just; He judges the wicked and protects His people.
- Key Verse: "The LORD is good, a refuge in times of trouble. He cares for those who trust in him." (Nahum 1:7)

## Structure of Nahum

1. The Character of God (Ch. 1)
    ◦ God is slow to anger but just in judgment.
    ◦ Assurance of protection for His people.
2. The Judgment of Nineveh (Ch. 2)
    ◦ Vivid description of Nineveh's fall.
3. The Guilt of Nineveh (Ch. 3)
    ◦ Reasons for judgment: cruelty, idolatry, arrogance.

## Key Themes of Nahum

1. God's Justice – He will judge nations for their violence and pride.
2. The End of Oppression – God brings down tyrants.
3. The Refuge of God – He is a stronghold for those who trust Him.
4. The Certainty of Judgment – God's patience has limits.
5. Comfort for God's People – His justice brings peace and deliverance.

## Exposition and Lessons

### *1. God's Character (Ch. 1)*

Nahum begins by declaring God's attributes: "The LORD is a jealous and avenging God; the LORD takes vengeance and is filled with wrath" (1:2). Yet he also declares: "The LORD is good, a refuge in times of trouble. He cares for those who trust in him" (1:7).

Lesson: God's justice and goodness go hand in hand. He punishes evil but protects His people.

## 2. *The Fall of Nineveh (Ch. 2)*

Nahum describes in detail the siege of Nineveh: chariots rushing, walls breached, treasures plundered, and the city left desolate. Though Assyria seemed invincible, God declared its end.

Lesson: No empire is too strong to fall when God decrees judgment.

## 3. *The Guilt of Nineveh (Ch. 3)*

Nahum lists Nineveh's sins: bloodshed, lies, plunder, prostitution, and sorcery. He mocks their false security: "All who hear the news about you clap their hands at your fall, for who has not felt your endless cruelty?" (3:19).

Lesson: Persistent sin invites inevitable destruction; God will not be mocked.

### Key Lessons from Nahum

1. God is patient but will not ignore sin forever.
2. Nations rise and fall under God's sovereignty.
3. Oppression and cruelty invite God's judgment.
4. God is a refuge for those who trust in Him.
5. Justice may seem delayed, but it is certain.

### Christ in Nahum

- God's Justice – Fulfilled in Christ, who will judge the nations with righteousness.
- The Refuge for His People (1:7) – Fulfilled in Christ, our shelter in times of trouble.
- The End of Tyranny – Fulfilled in Christ's victory over sin, death, and Satan.

- The Good News (1:15) – "Look, there on the mountains, the feet of one who brings good news" is fulfilled in Christ, the bringer of the Gospel.
- The Ultimate Deliverer – Fulfilled in Christ's kingdom of peace.

## Memory Verse

Nahum 1:7 – "The LORD is good, a refuge in times of trouble. He cares for those who trust in him."

## Reflection Questions

1. How does Nahum balance God's justice with His goodness?
2. What can we learn from Nineveh's downfall about pride and oppression?
3. How does Nahum comfort God's people in the face of powerful enemies?
4. What does it mean for God to be our refuge in times of trouble?
5. How does Nahum point us to Christ as our Deliverer?

## Final Exhortation

Students, Nahum teaches us that God's justice may take time, but it is certain. The mighty empire of Assyria seemed unstoppable, but it fell in a single generation because God decreed it.

For the wicked, Nahum is a warning: pride and cruelty will be judged. For the faithful, Nahum is a comfort: "The LORD is good, a refuge in times of trouble." In Christ, we see the perfect fulfillment of this truth—He is both the judge of sin and the refuge for all who trust in Him.

So let Nahum remind you: No oppressor is too strong, no injustice too great, and no sin too hidden for God's justice. And for those who belong to Christ, no trial is too heavy, for He is our refuge and strength.

# { 34 }

# Habakkuk

The book of Habakkuk is a unique and deeply personal dialogue between a prophet and God. Unlike other prophets, who mostly proclaimed God's word to the people, Habakkuk wrestled openly with God about the problem of evil and injustice.

He asked the questions we often ask: Why does God allow injustice? Why do the wicked prosper? Why does He sometimes use even more wicked people as instruments of judgment?

God's answers to Habakkuk remind us that He is sovereign, that His timing is perfect, and that "the righteous will live by faith" (Habakkuk 2:4). The book ends not with all the prophet's questions answered, but with a song of trust and praise in the God who saves.

Habakkuk teaches us how to move from confusion to faith, from complaint to worship, and from fear to joy.

## Background of Habakkuk

- Author: Habakkuk (meaning "to embrace" or "to wrestle").
- Date: ~605 BC, just before Babylon invaded Judah.
- Setting: Judah's moral decline and the looming threat of Babylon.
- Theme: Faith in God despite questions, doubts, and injustice.
- Key Verse: "The righteous will live by his faith." (Habakkuk 2:4)

## Structure of Habakkuk

1. Habakkuk's First Complaint (Ch. 1:1–4)
    ◦ Why does God tolerate injustice in Judah?
2. God's First Response (Ch. 1:5–11)
    ◦ Babylon will be the instrument of judgment.
3. Habakkuk's Second Complaint (Ch. 1:12–2:1)
    ◦ How can God use a wicked nation to punish His people?
4. God's Second Response (Ch. 2:2–20)
    ◦ The righteous live by faith.
    ◦ Woes against Babylon.
5. Habakkuk's Prayer and Song (Ch. 3)
    ◦ A vision of God's glory.
    ◦ A declaration of faith in God despite circumstances.

## Key Themes of Habakkuk

1. The Problem of Evil – Why does God allow injustice?
2. God's Sovereignty – He rules over nations and history.
3. Living by Faith – The righteous endure by trusting God.
4. The Certainty of Judgment – Evil will not prevail forever.
5. Joy in God – True faith rejoices even when circumstances are bleak.

## Exposition and Lessons

### 1. The Prophet's First Complaint (1:1–4)

Habakkuk laments the violence, injustice, and corruption in Judah: "How long, LORD, must I call for help, but you do not listen?" (1:2).

Lesson: It is not wrong to bring our questions and struggles honestly to God.

## 2. God's First Response (1:5–11)

God answers: He is raising up the Babylonians to bring judgment. But this confuses Habakkuk even more—how can God use a cruel, pagan nation to discipline His people?

Lesson: God's ways are higher than ours; His purposes often surprise us.

## 3. The Prophet's Second Complaint (1:12–2:1)

Habakkuk wrestles: "Why are you silent while the wicked swallow up those more righteous than themselves?" (1:13). He stations himself on the watchtower, waiting for God's reply.

Lesson: Faith waits on God for answers, even when His ways seem perplexing.

## 4. God's Second Response (2:2–20)

God tells Habakkuk to write the vision plainly: "The righteous will live by his faith" (2:4). He pronounces five "woes" against Babylon, promising that their arrogance, violence, and idolatry will be judged.

Lesson: The just live by trusting God's promises, not by sight.

## 5. Habakkuk's Prayer and Song (Ch. 3)

Habakkuk responds with a powerful prayer describing God's majesty and past deliverance. He ends with one of the greatest confessions of faith in Scripture: "Though the fig tree does not bud and there are no grapes on the vines... yet I will rejoice in the LORD, I will be joyful in God my Savior" (3:17–18).

Lesson: True faith worships God even when circumstances seem hopeless.

## Key Lessons from Habakkuk

1. It is okay to bring questions and doubts to God.
2. God's timing may seem slow, but His justice is sure.
3. The righteous live by faith, not by circumstances.
4. Arrogance and violence will ultimately be judged.
5. Joy is found not in circumstances but in God Himself.

## Christ in Habakkuk

- The Righteous Live by Faith (2:4) – Fulfilled in Christ and quoted in Romans 1:17, Galatians 3:11, and Hebrews 10:38.
- God's Justice – Fulfilled in Christ, who bore judgment for sin.
- The Glory of God (2:14) – "The earth will be filled with the knowledge of the glory of the LORD" points to Christ's reign.
- The God of Salvation (3:18) – Fulfilled in Christ, our Savior and source of joy.
- The Faithful Watchman – Habakkuk points to Christ, who perfectly trusted the Father.

## Memory Verse

Habakkuk 2:4 – "The righteous will live by his faith."

## Reflection Questions

1. What questions did Habakkuk ask God, and how are they relevant today?
2. How does God's response challenge human expectations?
3. What does it mean that "the righteous will live by faith"?
4. How does Habakkuk's song in chapter 3 model authentic worship?
5. How does this book point us forward to Christ and the gospel?

### Final Exhortation

Students, Habakkuk takes us on a journey from doubt to faith, from confusion to confidence, from complaint to worship. He teaches us that living by faith does not mean we understand everything—it means we trust God even when we do not.

When life seems unjust, when the wicked prosper, when God's timing feels slow, remember Habakkuk's confession: "Yet I will rejoice in the LORD, I will be joyful in God my Savior."

In Christ, we have even greater assurance. He is the fulfillment of Habakkuk's vision—the Righteous One who lived by faith and secured our salvation. Through Him, we can live with joy, no matter our circumstances.

{ 35 }

# Zephaniah

The book of Zephaniah is a powerful reminder of both the severity of God's judgment and the sweetness of His restoration. Zephaniah ministered during the reign of King Josiah, a time of religious reform in Judah. But beneath outward reform, the hearts of the people still wandered.

His prophecy focuses on the Day of the LORD—a day of judgment on Judah, on the nations, and on all creation. Yet Zephaniah does not end with despair. God promises to purify His people, restore them, and sing over them with joy.

Zephaniah helps us see that God's judgment is not meant to destroy but to cleanse and renew. His ultimate goal is a people who rejoice in Him as He rejoices over them.

## Background of Zephaniah

- Author: Zephaniah, great-great-grandson of King Hezekiah.
- Date: ~640–609 BC, during King Josiah's reign.
- Setting: Judah before Josiah's reforms fully took hold.
- Theme: The Day of the Lord brings judgment and restoration.
- Key Verse: "The LORD your God is with you, the Mighty Warrior who saves. He will take great delight in you; in his love he will no longer rebuke you, but will rejoice over you with singing." (Zephaniah 3:17)

## Structure of Zephaniah

1. Judgment on Judah (Ch. 1)
    ◦ Idolatry, complacency, and corruption condemned.
2. Judgment on the Nations (Ch. 2)
    ◦ God's justice extends beyond Israel.
3. Judgment and Hope for Jerusalem (Ch. 3:1–8)
    ◦ Leaders and people condemned.
    ◦ A remnant promised.
4. Promise of Restoration (Ch. 3:9–20)
    ◦ Purification of nations.
    ◦ God rejoices over His people.

## Key Themes of Zephaniah

1. The Day of the Lord – A day of judgment and salvation.
2. Universal Justice – God judges both His people and the nations.
3. God's Purifying Work – Judgment refines and restores.
4. The Joy of the Lord – God delights in His people.
5. Hope for the Remnant – A humble, faithful people will be restored.

## Exposition and Lessons

### 1. Judgment on Judah (Ch. 1)

Zephaniah warns Judah that the Day of the Lord is near: "The great day of the LORD is near—near and coming quickly" (1:14). He condemns idolatry, complacency, and those who say, "The LORD will do nothing, either good or bad" (1:12).

Lesson: Complacency and indifference toward God are just as dangerous as open rebellion.

## 2. Judgment on the Nations (Ch. 2)

God's judgment extends to Philistia, Moab, Ammon, Cush, and Assyria. Nineveh, once powerful, will become desolate.

Lesson: God is sovereign over all nations; no empire is beyond His reach.

## 3. Jerusalem's Corruption (Ch. 3:1–8)

Zephaniah denounces Jerusalem's leaders: prophets are arrogant, priests are corrupt, officials are like roaring lions. Yet God promises to leave a humble remnant who will trust in Him.

Lesson: Leadership without integrity invites God's judgment, but God preserves a faithful remnant.

## 4. The Joy of Restoration (Ch. 3:9–20)

The prophecy ends with breathtaking hope. God promises to purify the lips of the peoples so that all may call on His name. He will remove shame, restore fortunes, and most beautifully, rejoice over His people with singing (3:17).

Lesson: God's heart is not only to judge but to restore and delight in His people.

### Key Lessons from Zephaniah

1. The Day of the Lord is real and near—it calls us to repentance.
2. Complacency is spiritual danger; God calls us to wakefulness.
3. God judges all nations with justice and fairness.
4. God preserves a humble, faithful remnant.
5. God rejoices over His people with singing—His love is personal and joyful.

## Christ in Zephaniah

- The Day of the Lord – Fulfilled in Christ's first coming (judgment on sin at the cross) and second coming (final judgment and restoration).
- The Humble Remnant (3:12–13) – Fulfilled in Christ, who gathers a faithful people.
- The Joy of the Lord (3:17) – Fulfilled in Christ, who brings us into God's delight and love.
- The Purification of Nations (3:9) – Fulfilled at Pentecost, when all nations called on the name of the Lord.
- The Mighty Warrior Who Saves (3:17) – Fulfilled in Christ, who defeats sin and death.

## Memory Verse

Zephaniah 3:17 – "The LORD your God is with you, the Mighty Warrior who saves. He will take great delight in you; in his love he will no longer rebuke you, but will rejoice over you with singing."

## Reflection Questions

1. What forms of complacency do we see in Judah—and in our lives today?
2. How does Zephaniah show that God's justice is universal?
3. What hope does God give in promising a humble, faithful remnant?
4. How does Zephaniah 3:17 change our view of God's relationship with His people?
5. How does Christ fulfill the promises of Zephaniah?

## Final Exhortation

Students, Zephaniah reminds us that the Day of the Lord is both a warning and a promise. God's judgment is certain, but so is His restoration. He calls us out of complacency, purifies us from sin, and delights in us as His beloved people.

In Christ, these promises are fulfilled. He is the Mighty Warrior who saves, the one through whom God rejoices over us with singing. Let Zephaniah move you to repentance where needed, and then to joy, knowing that your God delights in you.

## { 36 }

# Haggai

The book of Haggai is one of encouragement and realignment. After returning from exile in Babylon, the people of Judah were discouraged. The temple of the Lord lay in ruins, while they busied themselves with building their own homes. Into this moment, God raised up Haggai to call the people back to their true priority—rebuilding the house of the Lord.

Haggai reminds us that God must be first. When His people put Him first, His blessing follows. The prophet also assures the people that the glory of the latter house will surpass the former, pointing us ultimately to Christ and His eternal kingdom.

### Background of Haggai

- Author: Haggai, the prophet.
- Date: 520 BC, during the reign of Darius I of Persia.
- Setting: Judah after the return from exile; the temple still in ruins.
- Theme: Put God first—rebuild His house and trust His promise of greater glory.
- Key Verse: "The glory of this present house will be greater than the glory of the former house, says the LORD Almighty. And in this place I will grant peace." (Haggai 2:9)

## Structure of Haggai

1. Call to Rebuild the Temple (Ch. 1)
   ◦ Rebuke for misplaced priorities.
   ◦ Call to action.
2. Encouragement for the Work (Ch. 2:1–9)
   ◦ God's presence with His people.
   ◦ Promise of greater glory.
3. Blessing Promised (Ch. 2:10–19)
   ◦ Holiness and obedience bring blessing.
4. Zerubbabel the Chosen Servant (Ch. 2:20–23)
   ◦ Promise of God's chosen leader.

## Key Themes of Haggai

1. God First – Our priorities must put God at the center.
2. The Presence of God – His Spirit strengthens and encourages.
3. The Glory of the Future Temple – A prophecy pointing to Christ.
4. Holiness and Blessing – Obedience brings God's favor.
5. God's Chosen Servant – Zerubbabel foreshadows Christ.

## Exposition and Lessons

### 1. Misplaced Priorities (Ch. 1)

The people said, "The time has not yet come to rebuild the LORD's house" (1:2). Meanwhile, they lived in paneled houses while the temple lay in ruins. Haggai confronts them: "Give careful thought to your ways" (1:5).

Lesson: When we neglect God's work for our own comfort, we miss His blessing.

## 2. *The Call to Rebuild (Ch. 1:12–15)*

The leaders and people obeyed the word of the Lord through Haggai. God stirred their spirits, and they began work on the temple.

Lesson: When God's people respond in obedience, He empowers them to do His will.

## 3. *Encouragement for the Workers (Ch. 2:1–9)*

Some were discouraged because the new temple seemed small compared to Solomon's. But God promised: "Be strong, for I am with you... The glory of this present house will be greater than the glory of the former house" (2:4, 9).

Lesson: God's presence is greater than outward appearances. His promise ensures greater glory.

## 4. *Holiness and Blessing (Ch. 2:10–19)*

Haggai teaches that holiness is not automatically transferred, but sin corrupts easily. God calls for holiness and promises blessing from the day they obey: "From this day on I will bless you" (2:19).

Lesson: God blesses obedience; holiness matters in all of life.

## 5. *Zerubbabel the Chosen Servant (Ch. 2:20–23)*

God tells Zerubbabel, governor of Judah, that He has chosen him as His signet ring, a symbol of authority and divine appointment. This points forward to the ultimate chosen servant—Jesus Christ.

Lesson: God's promises are fulfilled in Christ, the true Son of David.

### Key Lessons from Haggai

1. Put God first in your priorities.

2. God's presence gives strength to discouraged hearts.
3. The glory of Christ surpasses all outward glory.
4. Obedience and holiness invite God's blessing.
5. God's promises find their fulfillment in Christ, His chosen servant.

## Christ in Haggai

- The Greater Glory (2:9) – Fulfilled in Christ, who is the true temple of God (John 2:21).
- God's Presence – Fulfilled in Christ, "Immanuel—God with us."
- The Signet Ring (2:23) – Fulfilled in Christ, God's chosen ruler from David's line.
- Peace in the House of God (2:9) – Fulfilled in Christ, who is our peace.
- The True Temple – Fulfilled in Christ's body and the church as His dwelling place.

## Memory Verse

Haggai 2:9 – "The glory of this present house will be greater than the glory of the former house, says the LORD Almighty. And in this place I will grant peace."

## Reflection Questions

1. Why were the people slow to rebuild the temple, and how do we sometimes do the same today?
2. What does it mean to "give careful thought to your ways"?
3. How does God encourage discouraged workers in chapter 2?
4. Why is holiness important for experiencing God's blessing?
5. How does Haggai point us forward to Christ as the true temple and chosen servant?

### Final Exhortation

Students, Haggai's message is simple yet profound: put God first. The people of Judah lost focus, pursuing their own comfort while neglecting God's house. But when they obeyed, God's presence strengthened them, His blessing returned, and His promises gave them hope.

This message still speaks today. Christ is the greater glory, the true temple, and the chosen servant. When we align our lives with Him, God's blessing flows, and His peace fills His house.

So let Haggai encourage you: seek first the kingdom of God, and trust that the glory to come in Christ far outweighs anything this world can offer.

{ 37 }

# Zechariah

The book of Zechariah is one of the most hopeful and Christ-centered prophecies in the Old Testament. Written to the returning exiles alongside Haggai, it encourages God's people to rebuild the temple and look forward to the coming of the Messiah.

Through a series of visions, prophetic messages, and promises, Zechariah reveals God's plan for cleansing, restoration, and ultimate victory. The book contains some of the clearest prophecies about Christ's first and second coming, including His triumphal entry into Jerusalem, His betrayal for thirty pieces of silver, His pierced body, and His future reign as King of kings.

Zechariah reminds us that God's purposes are greater than immediate struggles. He points our eyes beyond present discouragement to the glory of Christ and His eternal kingdom.

## Background of Zechariah

- Author: Zechariah, priest and prophet.
- Date: ~520–518 BC (early visions), later sections possibly ~480 BC.
- Setting: Judah after the return from exile, facing discouragement about rebuilding the temple.
- Theme: God will restore His people and establish His kingdom through the coming Messiah.

- Key Verse: "'Not by might nor by power, but by my Spirit,' says the LORD Almighty." (Zechariah 4:6)

## Structure of Zechariah

1. Eight Night Visions (Ch. 1–6)
   - God's presence, cleansing, and protection.
   - Crowning of the priest-king.
2. Messages of Encouragement (Ch. 7–8)
   - Call to justice and mercy.
   - Promises of future blessing.
3. Prophecies of the Messiah (Ch. 9–14)
   - The coming King, betrayed and pierced.
   - Final victory and the Lord's reign.

## Key Themes of Zechariah

1. God's Spirit Empowers – Not human strength but the Spirit brings success.
2. Cleansing and Forgiveness – God removes sin and restores His people.
3. The Coming Messiah – Promises of Christ's suffering and glory.
4. God's Kingdom – His rule will extend to all nations.
5. Encouragement for the Discouraged – God's promises inspire hope.

## Exposition and Lessons

### 1. The Night Visions (Ch. 1–6)

Zechariah receives eight visions in a single night, full of symbolic imagery:

- A man among myrtle trees (God's presence with His people).

- Four horns and craftsmen (oppressors destroyed).
- A man with a measuring line (Jerusalem's restoration).
- Joshua the high priest cleansed (forgiveness of sins).
- The golden lampstand and olive trees (God's Spirit empowering).
- A flying scroll (judgment on sin).
- A woman in a basket (wickedness removed).
- Four chariots (God's sovereign power).

Lesson: God is present, cleansing, empowering, and ruling on behalf of His people.

## 2. The Priest-King (Ch. 6:9–15)

Joshua the high priest is crowned, symbolizing the coming of a priest-king who will unite spiritual and royal authority.

Lesson: Only Christ fulfills this perfectly as our High Priest and King.

## 3. Messages of Encouragement (Ch. 7–8)

The people ask about continuing their fasts. God replies that He desires justice, mercy, and compassion rather than empty rituals (7:9–10). He promises future blessing: "Old men and women will once again sit in the streets of Jerusalem... The city streets will be filled with boys and girls playing there" (8:4–5).

Lesson: God desires transformed hearts, not empty traditions. His future plans bring hope.

## 4. Prophecies of the Messiah (Ch. 9–14)

Zechariah's final chapters overflow with Messianic promises:

- "See, your king comes to you, righteous and victorious, lowly and riding on a donkey" (9:9).
- "They weighed out my wages, thirty pieces of silver" (11:12).
- "They will look on me, the one they have pierced" (12:10).
- The Shepherd struck and the sheep scattered (13:7).
- The Lord will return and be king over all the earth (14:9).

Lesson: Christ fulfills these prophecies in His first coming and will fulfill the rest at His return.

## Key Lessons from Zechariah

1. God's work is accomplished by His Spirit, not human strength.
2. God cleanses His people and removes their sin.
3. The Messiah is both priest and king.
4. Christ's first coming fulfilled many of Zechariah's prophecies.
5. Christ's second coming will establish His eternal kingdom.

## Christ in Zechariah

- The Cleansed High Priest (3:1–10) – Fulfilled in Christ, our great High Priest.
- The Branch (3:8; 6:12) – Fulfilled in Christ, the shoot from David's line.
- The Humble King (9:9) – Fulfilled in Christ's triumphal entry (Matthew 21:5).
- Thirty Pieces of Silver (11:12) – Fulfilled in Judas' betrayal of Christ.
- The Pierced One (12:10) – Fulfilled at the cross (John 19:37).
- The Struck Shepherd (13:7) – Fulfilled in Christ's arrest (Matthew 26:31).
- The Returning King (14:9) – Fulfilled when Christ comes again in glory.

## Memory Verse

Zechariah 4:6 – "So he said to me, 'This is the word of the LORD to Zerubbabel: Not by might nor by power, but by my Spirit,' says the LORD Almighty."

## Reflection Questions

1. How do Zechariah's visions encourage God's people to trust His presence and power?
2. Why is it significant that Christ is both priest and king?
3. Which Messianic prophecy in Zechariah strengthens your faith most?
4. How does Zechariah teach us to rely on God's Spirit rather than human strength?
5. What hope does Zechariah give us about Christ's return?

## Final Exhortation

Students, Zechariah lifts our eyes beyond immediate discouragement to God's glorious plan. His visions remind us that God is present, cleansing, empowering, and ruling for His people. His prophecies remind us that Christ came humbly the first time but will return in glory the second.

When you feel weak, remember: "Not by might nor by power, but by my Spirit." When you feel discouraged, remember: the King has come, and the King will come again. Let Zechariah's vision fuel your faith, your obedience, and your hope.

# Malachi

We now arrive at Malachi, the closing voice of the Old Testament. After this book, the prophetic word falls silent for 400 years until John the Baptist appears preparing the way for Christ. Malachi's message is therefore both a conclusion and a bridge.

The prophet confronts the people of Judah for their spiritual apathy. They were going through the motions of religion—offering sacrifices, keeping feasts—but their hearts were far from God. Malachi exposes their half-hearted worship, broken marriages, neglect of tithes, and doubts about God's justice.

Yet even in rebuke, Malachi shines with hope. God promises to send a messenger to prepare the way for the Lord, and the "sun of righteousness" will rise with healing in His wings. This is the promise of Christ, the fulfillment of God's covenant and the dawn of the New Testament.

## Background of Malachi

- Author: Malachi (name means "my messenger").
- Date: ~450–430 BC, after the rebuilding of the temple.
- Setting: Post-exilic Judah, outwardly religious but inwardly complacent.
- Theme: God rebukes spiritual apathy and calls His people to covenant faithfulness.

- Key Verse: "Return to me, and I will return to you," says the LORD Almighty. (Malachi 3:7)

## Structure of Malachi

1. God's Love Affirmed (Ch. 1:1–5)
    ◦ God's covenant love contrasted with Edom's judgment.
2. Rebukes Against the Priests (Ch. 1:6–2:9)
    ◦ Corrupt sacrifices and dishonorable worship.
3. Faithlessness of the People (Ch. 2:10–16)
    ◦ Broken marriages and covenant unfaithfulness.
4. The Coming Messenger and Day of the Lord (Ch. 2:17–3:6)
    ◦ God will purify His people.
5. Call to Return and Promise of Blessing (Ch. 3:7–12)
    ◦ Tithes and offerings restored.
6. The Book of Remembrance and Final Judgment (Ch. 3:13–4:6)
    ◦ Distinction between righteous and wicked.
    ◦ Promise of Elijah before the great Day of the Lord.

## Key Themes of Malachi

1. God's Covenant Love – He has not abandoned His people.
2. True Worship – God deserves honor, not half-hearted offerings.
3. Covenant Faithfulness – God calls for fidelity in marriage and in relationship with Him.
4. God's Justice – He will judge the wicked and vindicate the righteous.
5. The Coming Messenger – A prophecy of John the Baptist and Christ.

## Exposition and Lessons

### 1. God's Love Affirmed (1:1–5)

God begins by declaring His love: "I have loved you," says the LORD (1:2). Yet the people doubt His love. God points to His faithfulness to Israel contrasted with Edom's downfall.

Lesson: When we question God's love, we must remember His covenant faithfulness.

### 2. Corrupt Worship (1:6–2:9)

The priests dishonored God by offering blind, lame, and sick animals. God rebukes them for despising His name. He warns that He will not accept worship that is polluted.

Lesson: God deserves our best, not our leftovers. True worship honors His greatness.

### 3. Covenant Unfaithfulness (2:10–16)

The people profaned the covenant by marrying idolaters and by divorcing their wives without cause. God declares: "I hate divorce" (2:16), because it violates covenant faithfulness.

Lesson: Our relationships must reflect God's covenant loyalty.

### 4. The Coming Messenger (2:17–3:6)

The people doubted God's justice, asking, "Where is the God of justice?" (2:17). God promises to send His messenger to prepare the way. The Lord Himself will come to His temple like a refiner's fire.

Lesson: God's justice may seem delayed, but He will come to purify and judge.

## 5. Call to Return (3:7–12)

God calls His people: "Return to me, and I will return to you" (3:7). They had robbed Him by withholding tithes and offerings. He challenges them: "Test me in this… and see if I will not throw open the floodgates of heaven" (3:10).

Lesson: Faithfulness in giving reflects trust in God's provision and brings His blessing.

## 6. The Final Word (3:13–4:6)

God records a "scroll of remembrance" for those who fear Him. He promises that the wicked will be judged, but the righteous will rejoice: "The sun of righteousness will rise with healing in its wings" (4:2). Finally, He promises Elijah will come before the Day of the Lord—fulfilled in John the Baptist.

Lesson: God distinguishes between those who serve Him and those who do not. His final word is hope in the coming Messiah.

### Key Lessons from Malachi

1. God's love is faithful even when we doubt it.
2. Worship must be pure and wholehearted.
3. Covenant faithfulness in relationships honors God.
4. God's justice is certain, even if delayed.
5. Christ fulfills the promise of the coming messenger and the Sun of Righteousness.

### Christ in Malachi

- The Messenger of the Covenant (3:1) – Fulfilled in John the Baptist preparing the way for Christ.
- The Refiner's Fire (3:3) – Fulfilled in Christ, who purifies His people.

- The Sun of Righteousness (4:2) – Fulfilled in Christ, who brings healing and light.
- The Coming Judgment – Fulfilled in Christ's return.
- The Covenant Faithfulness – Fulfilled in Christ's unbreakable covenant of grace.

## Memory Verse

Malachi 3:7 – "Return to me, and I will return to you," says the LORD Almighty.

## Reflection Questions

1. Why did the people doubt God's love, and how does He prove it to them?
2. How does Malachi challenge us about the quality of our worship?
3. What does covenant faithfulness in marriage teach us about God's covenant?
4. How does Malachi's promise of the messenger prepare us for Christ?
5. How does the "sun of righteousness" point to Christ's healing work?

## Final Exhortation

Students, Malachi closes the Old Testament with a sobering but hopeful word. God rebukes half-hearted worship, broken faithfulness, and empty religion. Yet He also promises blessing, healing, and the coming of the Messiah.

As we step from Malachi into the silence before the New Testament, we are left waiting for the voice crying in the wilderness, the one who prepares the way of the Lord. That Lord is Christ—the Refiner, the Sun of Righteousness, the Messenger of the Covenant.

Let Malachi call you to wholehearted worship, faithful living, and eager anticipation of Christ's coming.

## Conclusion

We have now completed our journey through the 39 books of the Old Testament. Together, we have walked from the foundations of creation in Genesis to the final prophetic voice of Malachi. Along the way, we have seen the grand narrative of God's covenant love, His holiness, His justice, and His faithfulness to His people.

The Old Testament is not merely ancient history. It is the living word of God, written to teach, correct, and equip us for life today. Each book, from the Law to the Prophets, points us forward to the Messiah—Jesus Christ—who fulfills every promise of God.

1. Genesis–Deuteronomy (The Law) – God created, called Abraham, delivered His people from Egypt, and gave His covenant law.
2. Joshua–Esther (The History) – God brought His people into the land, established kingship, and preserved His people through exile and return.
3. Job–Song of Songs (The Poetry & Wisdom) – God revealed wisdom for life, worship through Psalms, and reflections on suffering, love, and meaning.
4. Isaiah–Malachi (The Prophets) – God warned of judgment, called His people to repentance, and promised hope in the coming Messiah.

Together, these books give us the foundation of our faith and prepare us for the arrival of Christ.

## Key Lessons from the Old Testament

- God is Creator and King – He rules over all creation and history.
- God is Holy – He calls His people to live in covenant faithfulness.
- Sin Brings Judgment – Disobedience leads to ruin, but God is merciful.
- God's Love is Relentless – Like Hosea's love for Gomer, God pursues His people.
- The Messiah is Promised – From Genesis to Malachi, Christ is foreshadowed as Savior, King, and Deliverer.

## Christ Throughout the Old Testament

Every book whispers His name:

- In Genesis, He is the Seed of the Woman.
- In Exodus, the Passover Lamb.
- In Leviticus, the Great High Priest.
- In Numbers, the Bronze Serpent lifted up.
- In Deuteronomy, the Prophet greater than Moses.
- In the Prophets, the Coming King and Suffering Servant.
- In the Psalms, our Shepherd and Savior.
- In Malachi, the Sun of Righteousness who rises with healing in His wings.

The Old Testament is incomplete without Him, and the New Testament cannot be understood apart from these foundations.

## Final Reflection

As you close this book, remember: the Old Testament is not simply about Israel's story—it is about God's story. A story that leads to Christ and includes you.

The lessons of obedience, faith, justice, mercy, and covenant love are not relics of the past; they are guiding truths for today. May this survey give you a hunger to study the Scriptures more deeply, to hear God's voice more clearly, and to live in greater faithfulness to Him.

## Final Exhortation

Students, the Old Testament ends with anticipation. Malachi leaves us looking forward to the coming of the Messenger and the Lord Himself. That silence is broken in the New Testament with the cry of John the Baptist: "Prepare the way for the Lord."

And the Lord came—Jesus Christ, the fulfillment of every prophecy, the answer to every promise, the Savior of the world.

So I urge you: do not let this be the end of your study, but the beginning of a deeper walk with Christ. Read the Scriptures with eyes open to see Him, hearts open to love Him, and lives surrendered to serve Him.

For truly, all of Scripture declares: The kingdom is the Lord's, and He shall reign forever and ever.

Dr. Tony Medley Sr. is a pastor, teacher, mentor, and author whose life and ministry have been dedicated to helping people discover the power of God's Word spoken over their lives. Known for his passionate preaching and practical teaching, Dr. Medley has spent decades equipping believers to hear God's voice, walk in their identity in Christ, and live with purpose and bold faith. His ministry extends beyond the pulpit—through books, training materials, stage plays, and discipleship resources—designed to ignite transformation in individuals, churches, and communities.

Dr. Medley combines deep biblical insight with everyday application, ensuring that readers not only understand the Scriptures but also live them out with confidence. With a message that is both prophetic and practical, Dr. Medley inspires people to see themselves through heaven's perspective. He believes every person is "wrapped in the conversation" of God and destined to thrive in His promises.

When he is not writing or teaching, Dr. Medley is serving his church family, mentoring emerging leaders, and enjoying time with his own family, who remain his greatest earthly joy.

www.ingramcontent.com/pod-product-compliance
Lightning Source LLC
Chambersburg PA
CBHW050441150626
46551CB00028B/938